A Little Argument

Second Edition

Lester Faigley
University of Texas at Austin

Jack Selzer
Penn State University

Boston Columbus Indianapolis New York San Francisco Upper Saddle River
Amsterdam CapeTown Dubai London Madrid Milan Munich Paris Montréal Toronto
Delhi Mexico City São Paulo Sydney Hong Kong Seoul Singapore Taipei Tokyo

Editor in Chief: Joe Opiela
Senior Acquisitions Editor: Brad Potthoff
Senior Marketing Manager:
  Sandra McGuire
Editorial Assistant: Lauren Cunningham
Production Project Manager:
  Romaine Denis
Project Coordination, Text Design,
  and Electronic Page Makeup:
  Abinaya Rajendran,
  Integra Software Services, Ltd.

Creative Director: Jayne Conte
Cover Designer: Suzanne
  Behnke
Photo Researcher: Jorgensen
  Fernandez
Printer/Binder: Courier
  Corporation—Westford
Cover Printer: Courier
  Corporation—Westford

Unless otherwise credited, all photos Copyright © Lester Faigley Photos.

Library of Congress Cataloging-in-Publication Data
Faigley, Lester
  A little argument/Lester Faigley, Jack Selzer.—2nd ed.
    p. cm.
  Includes index.
  ISBN-13: 978-0-321-85276-2 (alk. paper)
  ISBN-10: 0-321-85276-1 (alk. paper)
    1. English language—Rhetoric—Problems, exercises, etc.
2. Persuasion (Rhetoric)—Problems, exercises, etc. 3. Academic
writing. I. Selzer, Jack. II. Title.
  PE1431.F37 2013
  808'.042—dc23
                                                    2012017710

10 9 8 7 6 5 4 3 —CW—15 14 13

PEARSON

ISBN-10:   0-321-85276-1
ISBN-13: 978-0-321-85276-2

Contents

Introduction

Nothing you learn in college will prove to be more important to you than the ability to write an effective argument.

You're already aware that campus life is itself filled with arguments. There are hot-button public issues that are always engaging the academic community—binge drinking, for example, or making the university more environmentally sustainable, or improving this or that athletic team, or how to invest university resources most appropriately, or how to improve campus housing or study-abroad opportunities. Meanwhile, in the classroom and in their research programs, faculty members present arguments on current controversies such as climate change and economic policy as well as on more scholarly topics such as the workings of evolution, the dynamics of Ralph Ellison's fiction, or the means of determining the material composition of the planet Mercury.

After college you will particularly need to communicate your ideas and point of view effectively. Your livelihood and your engagement in the community will depend on it. Sometimes as a citizen you will be moved to register your views on the local school system or local downtown development; or as a member of a church or synagogue or a civic organization, you will be suggesting ways of making a positive difference. And certainly in the workplace you will often be defending your ideas and point of view, whether you are working as an engineer to develop a more efficient transit system for a client or as a business manager to recommend improved office procedures or sales tactics. Arguments are everywhere, it seems—in e-mails, on Web sites, in magazines and newspapers, in the reports and sales documents and advertisements of scientists, public relations professionals, government workers, lawyers, and educators.

A Little Argument will give you a set of rules of thumb that you can use in school and after in order to mount effective arguments. For a number of years we have studied arguments, taught students how to argue, and have listened to others talk and write about the art of persuasion. What we have found is that while there is no simple recipe for effective arguments, there are strategies and tactics that you can rely on in almost any situation to ensure that your ideas are considered seriously. You'll find these strategies and tactics explained with examples in these chapters.

Chapter 1: Making an Effective Argument

You'll find out what exactly is an argument (hint: it's not about obliterating other points of view), what readers expect in a written argument in college, and how you can increase your credibility.

Chapter 2: Analyzing an Argument

Knowing how to analyze arguments, both verbal and visual ones, helps you to become a stronger writer of arguments.

Chapter 3: Writing an Argument

Finding a topic and exploring that topic are the keys to getting started. Finding evidence to support your reasons, understanding your audience, and organizing your argument effectively are the keys to success.

Chapter 4: Constructing an Argument

You'll learn how to build five of the most common kinds of arguments: definition arguments, causal arguments, evaluation arguments, rebuttal arguments, and proposal arguments.

Chapter 5: Researching an Argument

Chapter 5 guides you in identifying a subject to research; in gathering information using field research, the Web, and library sources; and in evaluating the sources of information you discover.

Chapter 6: Documenting an Argument

Chapter 6 explains how to document appropriately and credibly the sources you use and how to avoid plagiarism.

Chapter 7: Revising an Argument

The final chapter shows you how to evaluate your draft and how to improve it significantly by revising.

1

Making an Effective Argument

WHAT EXACTLY IS AN ARGUMENT?

One of the best-known celebrities on YouTube is an anonymous video director who wears a Guy Fawkes mask and uses the name MadV. In November 2006 he posted a short video in which he held up his hand with the words "One World" written on his palm and invited viewers to take a stand by uploading a video to YouTube. They responded by the thousands, writing short messages written on their palms. MadV then compiled many of the responses in a 4-minute video titled "The Message" and posted it on YouTube.

MadV's project has been praised as a celebration of the values of the YouTube community. The common theme that we all should try to love and better understand other people is one that few oppose. Yet the video also raises the question of how any of the goals might be achieved. One hand reads "Stop Bigotry." We see a great deal of hatred in written responses to many YouTube videos. What might lessen the hatred? Slogans like "Open Mind," "Be Colorblind," "Love Is Stronger," "No More Racism," and "Yup One World" seem inadequate for the scope of the problem.

Like the ink-on-hand messages, bumper stickers usually consist of unilateral statements ("Be Green," "Save the Whales," or "Share the Road") but provide no supporting evidence or reasons for why anyone should do what they say. People committed to a particular cause or belief often assume that their reasons are self-evident, and that everyone thinks the same way. These writers know they can count on certain words and phrases to produce predictable responses.

In college courses, in public life, and in professional careers, however, written arguments cannot be reduced to signs or slogans. Writers of effective arguments do not assume that everyone thinks the same way or holds the same beliefs. They attempt to change people's minds by convincing them of the validity of new ideas or the superiority of a particular course of action. Writers of such arguments not only offer evidence and reasons to support their position but also examine the assumptions on which an argument is based, address opposing arguments, and anticipate their readers' objections.

Extended written arguments make more demands on their readers than most other kinds of writing. Like bumper stickers, these arguments often appeal to our emotions. But they typically do much more.

- They expand our knowledge with the depth of their analysis.

- They lead us through a complex set of claims by providing networks of logical relationships and appropriate evidence.

- They build on what has been written previously by providing trails of sources.

- Finally, they cause us to reflect on what we read, in a process that we will shortly describe as critical reading.

WRITING ARGUMENTS IN COLLEGE

Writing in college varies considerably from course to course. A lab report for a biology course looks quite different from a paper in your English class, just as a classroom observation in an education course differs from a case study report in an accounting class.

Nevertheless, much of the writing you will do in college consists of making successful arguments. Some common expectations about effective arguments extend across disciplines. For example, you could be assigned to write a proposal for a downtown light-rail system in a number of different classes—civil engineering, urban planning, government, or management. The emphasis of such a proposal would change depending on the course. In all cases, however, the proposal would require a complex argument in which you describe the problem that the light-rail system would solve, make a specific proposal that addresses the problem, explain the benefits of the system, estimate the cost, identify funding sources, assess alternatives to your plan, and anticipate possible opposition. It's a lot to think about.

Setting out a specific proposal or claim supported by reasons and evidence is at the heart of most college writing, no matter what the course. Some expectations of arguments (such as including a thesis statement) may be familiar to you, but others (such as the emphasis on finding alternative ways of thinking about a subject and finding facts that might run counter to your conclusions) may be unfamiliar.

WRITTEN ARGUMENTS...	WRITERS ARE EXPECTED TO...
State explicit claims	Make a claim that isn't obvious. The main claim is often called a **thesis**.
Support claims with reasons	Express reasons in a **because clause** after the claim (We should do something *because* _____).
Base reasons on evidence	Provide evidence for reasons in the form of facts, statistics, testimony from reliable sources, and direct observations.
Consider opposing positions	Help readers understand why there are disagreements about issues by accurately representing differing views.
Analyze with insight	Provide in-depth analysis of what they read and view.
Investigate complexity	Explore the complexity of a subject by asking, "Have you thought about this?" or "What if you discard the usual way of thinking about a subject and take the opposite point of view?"
Organize information clearly	Make the major parts evident to readers and indicate which parts are subordinate to others.
Signal relationships of parts	Indicate logical relationships clearly so that readers can follow an argument without getting lost.
Document sources carefully	Provide the sources of information so that readers can consult the same sources the writer used.

How Can You Argue Responsibly?

In Washington, D.C., cars with diplomatic license plates are often parked illegally. Their drivers know they will not be towed or ticketed. People who abuse the diplomatic privilege are announcing, "I'm not playing by the rules."

When you begin an argument by saying, "in my opinion," you are making a similar announcement. First, the phrase is redundant. A reader assumes that if you make a claim in writing, you believe that claim. More important, a claim is rarely *only* your opinion. Most beliefs and assumptions are shared by many people. If a claim truly is only your opinion, it can be easily dismissed. If your position is likely to be held by at least a few other people, however, then a responsible reader must consider your position seriously. You argue responsibly when you set out the reasons for making a claim, offer facts to support those reasons, and acknowledge that other people may have positions different from yours.

How Can You Argue Respectfully?

Our culture is competitive, and our goal often is to win. Professional athletes, top trial lawyers, and candidates for president of the United States either win big or lose. But most of us live in a world in which our opponents don't go away when the game is over.

Most of us have to deal with people who disagree with us at times but continue to work and live in our communities. The idea of winning in such situations can only be temporary. Soon enough, we will need the support of those who were on the other side of the most recent issue.

Usually, listeners and readers are more willing to consider your argument seriously if you cast yourself as a respectful partner rather than as a competitor. Put forth your arguments in the spirit of mutual support and negotiation—in the interest of finding the *best* way, not "my way." How can you be the person that your reader will want to join rather than resist? Here are a few suggestions both for writing arguments and for discussing controversial issues.

- **Try to think of yourself as engaged not so much in winning over your audience as in courting your audience's cooperation.** Argue vigorously, but not so vigorously that opposing views are vanquished or silenced. Remember that your goal is to invite a response that creates a dialogue.

- **Show that you understand and genuinely respect your listener's or reader's position even if you think the position is ultimately wrong.** Remember to argue against opponents' positions, not against the opponents themselves. Arguing respectfully often means representing an opponent's position in terms that he or she would accept. Look for ground that you already share with your opponent, and search for even more. See yourself as a mediator. Consider that neither you nor the other person has arrived at the best solution. Then carry on in the hope that dialogue will lead to an even better course of action than the one you now recommend.

- **Cultivate a sense of humor and a distinctive voice.** Many textbooks about argument emphasize using a reasonable voice. But a reasonable voice doesn't have to be a dull one. Humor is a legitimate tool of argument. Although playing an issue strictly for laughs risks not being taken seriously, nothing creates a sense of goodwill quite as much as tasteful humor. A sense of humor can be especially welcome when the stakes are high, sides have been chosen, and tempers are flaring.

Consider your argument as just one move in a larger process that might end up helping you. Most times we argue because we think we have something to offer. However, realize that you might learn something during your research and discussion in the course of developing and presenting your views. You might even change your mind. Holding on to that attitude will keep you from becoming too overbearing and dogmatic.

THINK ABOUT YOUR CREDIBILITY

A few writers begin with instant credibility because of what they have accomplished. For example, if you're a tennis player, likely you will pay attention to advice from Serena Williams. But if you are like most of the rest of us, you don't have instant credibility.

Think About How You Want Your Readers to See You

To get your readers to take you seriously, you must convince them that they can trust you. You need to get them to see you as

- **Concerned.** Readers want you to be committed to what you are writing about. They also expect you to be concerned with them as readers. After all, if you don't care about them, why should they read what you write?

- **Well informed.** Many people ramble on about any subject without knowing anything about it. If they are family members, you have to suffer their opinions, but it is not enjoyable. College writing requires that you do your homework on a subject.

- **Fair.** Many writers look at only one side of an issue. Readers respect objectivity and an unbiased approach.

- **Ethical.** Many writers use only the facts that support their positions and often distort facts and sources. Critical readers often notice what is being left out. Don't try to conceal what doesn't support your position.

Build Your Credibility

Know what's at stake. What you are writing about should matter to your readers. If its importance is not evident, it's your job to explain why your readers should consider it important.

LESS EFFECTIVE:
We should be concerned about two-thirds of Central and South America's 110 brightly colored harlequin frog species becoming extinct in the last twenty years. (*The loss of any species is unfortunate, but the writer gives us no other reason for concern.*)

MORE EFFECTIVE:
The rapid decline of amphibians world-wide due to global warming may be the advance warning of the loss of cold-weather species such as polar bears, penguins, and reindeer.

Have your readers in mind. If you are writing about a specialized subject that

LESS EFFECTIVE:
Reduction in the value of a debt security, especially a bond, results from a rise

your readers don't know much about, take the time to explain key concepts.

in interest rates. Conversely, a decline in interest rates results in an increase in the value of a debt security, especially bonds. (*The basic idea is here, but it is not expressed clearly, especially if the reader is not familiar with investing.*)

MORE EFFECTIVE:
Bond prices move inversely to interest rates. When interest rates go up, bond prices go down, and when interest rates go down, bond prices go up.

Think about alternative solutions and points of view. Readers appreciate a writer's ability to see a subject from multiple perspectives.

LESS EFFECTIVE:
We will reduce greenhouse gas and global warming only if we greatly increase wind-generated electricity. (*Wind power is an alternative energy source, but it is expensive and many people don't want windmills in scenic areas. The writer also doesn't mention using energy more efficiently.*)

MORE EFFECTIVE:
If the world is serious about limiting carbon emissions to reduce global warming, then along with increasing efficient energy use, all non–carbon emitting energy sources must be considered, including nuclear power. Nuclear power now produces about 20 percent of U.S. electricity with no emissions—the equivalent of taking 58 million passenger cars off the road.

Be honest. Readers also appreciate writers who admit what they aren't sure about. Leaving readers with unanswered questions can lead them to think further about your subject.

LESS EFFECTIVE:
The decline in violent crime during the 1990s was due to putting more people in jail with longer sentences.

MORE EFFECTIVE:
Exactly what caused the decline in violent crime during the 1990s remains uncertain. Politicians point to longer sentences for criminals, but the decrease in the population most likely to commit crimes—the 16-to-35 age group—may have been a contributing factor.

A CASE STUDY: THE MICROCREDIT DEBATE

Two women financed by microcredit sell scarves in Quito, Ecuador.

World Bank researchers reported in 2009 that 1.4 billion people—over 20 percent of the 6.7 billion people on earth—live below the extreme poverty line of $1.25 a day, with 6 million children starving to death every year. One cause of continuing extreme poverty is the inability of poor people to borrow money because they have no cash income or assets. Banks have seldom made loans to very poor people, who have had to turn to moneylenders that charge high interest rates, sometimes exceeding 100 percent a month.

In 1976, Muhammad Yunus observed that poor women in Bangladesh who made bamboo furniture could not profit from their labor because they had to borrow money at high interest rates to buy bamboo. Yunus loaned $27 to forty-two women out of his pocket. They repaid him at an interest rate of two cents per loan. The success of the experiment eventually led to Yunus securing a loan from the government to create a bank to make loans to poor people. The Grameen Bank (Village Bank) became a model for other microfinancing projects in Bangladesh, serving 7 million people, 94 percent of whom are women. For his work with the Grameen initiative, Yunus received the Nobel Peace Prize in 2006.

The conversation about microcredit has led others to put new ideas on the table.

Microcredit now has many supporters, including Hollywood stars like Natalie Portman and Michael Douglas, companies like Benetton and Sam's Club, and former president Bill Clinton. But the success in Bangladesh has not been replicated in many other poor countries. Many critics point to the shortcomings of microcredit. This debate can be better understood if you consider the different points of view on microcredit to be different voices in a conversation.

Mapping a conversation like the debate about microcredit often can help you identify how you can add to the conversation. What can you add to what's been said?

Some people claim that _____.

Other people respond that _____.

Still others claim that _____.

I agree with X's and Y's points, but I maintain that _____

because _____.

2

Analyzing an Argument

WHAT IS RHETORICAL ANALYSIS?

To many people, the term *rhetoric* suggests speech or writing that is highly ornamental or deceptive or manipulative. You might hear someone say, "That politician is just using a bunch of rhetoric" or "The rhetoric of that advertisement is very deceiving." But *rhetoric* is also used these days in a positive or neutral sense to describe human communication; for instance, *"Silent Spring* is one of the most influential pieces of environmental rhetoric ever written." When we study rhetoric, we usually associate it with effective communication, following Aristotle's classic definition of rhetoric as "the art of finding in any given case the available means of persuasion."

Rhetoric is not just a means of *producing* effective communication. It is also a way of *understanding* communication. The two aspects mutually support one another: becoming a better writer makes you a better interpreter, and becoming a better interpreter makes you a better writer.

Rhetorical analysis is the effort to understand how people attempt to influence others through language and more broadly through every kind of symbolic action—not only speeches, articles, and books, but also architecture, movies, television shows, memorials, Web sites, advertisements, photos and other images, dance, and popular songs. It might be helpful to think of rhetorical analysis as a kind of critical reading. Critical reading—rhetorical analysis, that is—involves studying carefully any kind of persuasive action in order to understand it better and to appreciate the tactics that it uses. Doing a rhetorical analysis can help you to understand arguments by others and improve your ability to argue effectively yourself.

BUILD A RHETORICAL ANALYSIS

Rhetorical analysis examines how an idea is shaped and presented to an audience in a particular form for a specific purpose. There are many approaches to rhetorical analysis and no one "correct" way to do it. Generally, though, approaches to rhetorical analysis can be placed between two broad extremes—not mutually exclusive categories but extremes at the ends of a continuum.

At one end of the continuum are analyses that concentrate more on **texts** than on contexts. They typically use rhetorical concepts and terminologies to analyze the features of texts. Let's call this approach **textual analysis**. At the other extreme are approaches that emphasize **context** over text. These focus on reconstructing the cultural environment, or context, that existed when a particular rhetorical event took place. That reconstruction provides clues about the persuasive tactics and appeals. Those who undertake **contextual analysis** regard particular rhetorical acts as parts of larger communicative chains, or "conversations."

Now let's examine these two approaches in detail.

ANALYZE THE RHETORICAL FEATURES: TEXTUAL ANALYSIS

Just as expert teachers in every field of endeavor—from baseball to biology—devise vocabularies to facilitate specialized study, rhetoricians too have developed a set of key concepts to describe rhetorical activities. A fundamental concept in rhetoric is audience: according to the concept of *decorum*, or "appropriateness," everything within an effective persuasive act—everything from content choices through minor stylistic matters—develops from a central rhetorical goal that governs consistent choices that are based on occasion and audience. In addition, terms like *ethos, pathos,* and *logos*, all associated with invention, account for features of texts related to the trustworthiness and credibility of the writer or speaker (ethos), for the persuasive good reasons in an argument that derive from a community's mostly deeply held values (pathos), and for the good reasons that emerge from intellectual reasoning (logos). Rhetoricians also attend

The statue of Castor stands at the entrance of the Piazza del Campidoglio in Rome. A textual analysis focuses on the statue itself. The size and realism of the statue makes it a masterpiece of classical Roman sculpture.

to arrangement (or organization) as well as style (i.e., word choices and sentence structures).

An example will make textual rhetorical analysis clearer. Let's look at the "Statement on the Articles of Impeachment" by Barbara Jordan at the end of this chapter, and the student rhetorical analysis that follows it (pp. 33–42). In the pages that follow, we use the fundamental concepts of rhetoric to better understand the presentation by Barbara Jordan.

Jordan's Purpose and Argument

What is the purpose of Jordan's speech? She wrote it in 1974, but it remains compellingly readable still because it concerns a perennial (and very contemporary) American issue: the limits of presidential power.

A contextual analysis focuses on the surroundings and history of the statue. According to legend, Castor (left of staircase) and his twin brother Pollux (right of staircase), the mythical sons of Leda, assisted Romans in an early battle. Romans built a large temple in the Forum to honor them. The statues were discovered in the sixteenth century and in 1583 were brought to stand at the top of the Cordonata, a staircase designed by Michelangelo as part of a renovation of the Piazza del Campidoglio commissioned by Pope Paul III Farnese in 1536.

In this case, Jordan argues in favor of bringing articles of impeachment against President Richard Nixon. She feels that the drastic step of impeachment is called for because President Nixon had violated the Constitution. Essentially Jordan's argument comes down to this: Nixon, like any abuser of the Constitution, should be removed from office because he has been guilty of causing "the dimunition, the subversion, the destruction, of the Constitution" (para. 3). The Founders of the nation established clear grounds for impeachment, and Nixon trespassed on those grounds by covering up crimes and by stonewalling efforts to investigate misdeeds. He "committed offenses, and planned and directed and acquiesced in a course of conduct which the Constitution will not tolerate" (para. 20). Jordan's speech amounts to a definition of impeachment in general, based on the Constitution, which then calls for President Nixon's impeachment in particular.

Jordan's Use of Logos, Pathos, and Ethos

Logos

Jordan constructs her case in favor of impeachment through a carefully reasoned process. She begins by presenting a patient account of the meaning of impeachment as it appears in the Constitution, on which her "faith is whole; it is complete; it is total" (para. 3). The Constitution defines impeachment not as conviction but as a kind of indictment of a president for misconduct; once a president is impeached, a trial then follows, conducted by the House of Representatives and judged by the Senate. Only after conviction by two-thirds of the senators, after a fair trial, could the president be removed. The Constitution offers grounds for impeachment only on very general terms: Article III, section 4, explains that presidents can be removed from office for treason, bribery, or other high crimes and misdemeanors.

Do Nixon's actions qualify as impeachable? Jordan must refer to the statements that the Founders made during the ratification process for the Constitution to lay out exactly what might be considered an impeachable high crime. After a lengthy explanation of what qualifies as impeachable—"the misconduct of public men" only in "occasional and extraordinary cases," and only "if the President be connected in any suspicious manner with any person and there [are] grounds to believe he will shelter him," and only if there are "great misdemeanors" and not simple "maladministration"—she then applies the definition to Nixon's actions. Carefully and systematically she offers the evidence. She ties "misconduct," the cover-up of crimes, and the sanctioning of other misdeeds to Nixon: "the President had knowledge that these funds were being paid" (para. 15); he consorted with a range of suspicious characters and "knew about the break-in of the psychiatrist's office" (para. 16); and he "engaged in a series of public statements and actions designed to thwart the lawful investigation of government prosecutors" (para. 17). The conclusion follows rationally and inevitably. The president must be impeached. Note how the third paragraph of Jonathan Jackson's analysis at the end of the chapter addresses issues of logos in Jordan's speech.

Pathos

The logical appeals in Jordan's speech are reinforced by her emotional appeals. Her repeated references to the Constitution have a strong emotional appeal. Because Americans have a deep respect for the Constitution, any attempt to undermine it must be resisted firmly and forcefully.

Perhaps the speech's most powerful emotional moment comes in the second paragraph. By bringing up the famous "We the people" opening of the Constitution early in the speech, Jordan rouses passions and brings listeners to her side. She calls attention to how she as an African American woman was originally left out of the Constitution because it defined citizens only as white males. The appeal to fair play certainly rouses emotions in her listeners; it gains considerable sympathy for Jordan.

You can probably note many other points in the speech that carry an emotional dimension. Jordan concludes her speech by rightly saying, "it is reason, and not passion, which must guide our deliberations, guide our debate, and guide our decision." But she also brings considerable pathos to bear on her argument. Jordan appeals to the whole person.

Ethos

Why do we take Jordan's word about the legal precedents and evidence that she cites? It is because she establishes her *ethos*, or trustworthiness, early in the essay and sustains it throughout. Again, note how Jonathan Jackson's essay attends to ethos, particularly in his fourth paragraph. There he commends Jordan's scholarship, which establishes her credibility as a lawyer, and notes her credibility as a citizen, which derives from her position as an African American woman. Jordan comes through as a thorough professional, as an educated lawyer who has studied constitutional law and has done her homework, and as a deeply concerned citizen. Consequently, we can trust her word and trust her judgment. Particularly effective is her citation of the historical record on impeachment. She has sifted the records to draw from the most respected of the framers of the Constitution—notably James Madison—and from authorities later in our national history. She buttresses her trustworthiness in other ways too:

- She quotes widely, if unobtrusively: by using precise quotations, she adds a trustworthy scholarly dimension to her presentation.
- She touches lightly on her own status as an African American woman to lend firsthand authority to what she has to say.
- She demonstrates a knowledge of history and constitutional law.
- She connects herself to America generally by linking herself to traditional American values such as freedom, ethnic pride, fair play, and tolerance.

Jordan knew that Nixon's supporters were depending on being able to make the case against Nixon into a partisan matter, Democrats vs. Republicans. So in her speech Jordan goes to great length to avoid being placed in a partisan camp and to be regarded as fair-minded. Overall, she comes off as hard working, honest, educated, and patriotic. And definitely credible.

Jordan's Arrangement

We have already said some things about the arrangement of Jordan's speech. We especially noted how the overall structure follows the pattern of most definition arguments: Jordan offers her definition of impeachment and then in the final third of the talk applies that definition to the case of Richard Nixon. Note how she begins with an introductory comment about her personal situation; the tone of the first few sentences is light hearted as she offers gentle humor to "Mr. Chairman." And then she turns to a personal anecdote about her being left out of the Constitution "by mistake." In many ways, then, Jordan organizes very conventionally—she has a clear beginning, middle, and end.

And yet in other ways the arrangement is not so conventional. Rather than sticking with a light tone, Jordan turns deadly serious in paragraph 3. In the manner of a lawyer stating a legal case, a lawyer offering a final argument after evidence has been heard, she announces that her presentation will be based solely on constitutional law, and then follows with point after point of a formal legal brief in favor of impeachment. Note that Jordan does not announce her conclusion early; just as if she were addressing a jury, she postpones her thesis ("If the impeachment provision in the Constitution will not reach the offenses charged here, then perhaps that 18th-century Constitution should be abandoned to a 20th-century paper shredder": para. 19) until the very end. Had she begun with such an explicit statement of her thesis, had she begun by stating her conclusion early, her speech might have been dismissed as a partisan speech and not a legal case.

Jordan's Style

What about Jordan's style? How is it appropriate to her purposes? Would you describe it as "lawyerly" or not?

In one sense, Jordan speaks very much as a lawyer would speak to other lawyers. Her fourth paragraph, for example, consists solely of legal language, so legal that it is difficult for a lay person to understand where these quotations come from and what they mean. And further quotations from law cases show up as the speech continues. It is as if Jordan is addressing lawyers because she repeatedly uses legal terminology: "proceed forthwith"; "obfuscation"; "the powers relating to impeachment are an essential check in the hands of the body of the legislature against and upon the encroachments of the executive"; "the framers confided in the Congress the power, if need be, to remove the President"; "a narrowly channeled exception to the separation-of-powers maxim"; and so on.

And yet in another sense, Jordan is speaking in an accessible way to a larger audience of all Americans. Rather than sustain the legal language, she speaks in simple sentences and simple cadences from beginning to the very end—from "Today I am an inquisitor.... My faith in the Constitution is whole, it is complete, it is total" to "That's the question. We know that. We know the question.... It is reason, not passion, which must guide our deliberations, guide our debate, and guide our decision." Whenever legal jargon threatens to take over, Jordan returns to everyday language accessible to all: "The Constitution doesn't say that"; "they [the framers] did not make the accusers and the judgers the same person"; "we are trying to be big because the task before us is a big one"; "we know the nature of impeachment. We've been talking of it awhile now." In sum, Jordan's style is in keeping with her ethos. Because she wishes to come off as both a concerned citizen and a legal expert, she chooses a style that is one part newspaper reporting—simple, straightforward, unadorned—and one part legal brief—technical and jargony, full of convolutions and qualifications.

There is more to say about the rhetorical choices that Jordan made in crafting her "Statement on the Articles of Impeachment," but this analysis is enough to illustrate our main point. Textual rhetorical analysis employs rhetorical terminology—in this case, terms borrowed from the rhetorical tradition such as *ethos, pathos, logos, arrangement, style,* and *tone*—as a way of helping us to understand how a writer makes choices to achieve certain effects. And textual analysis cooperates with contextual analysis.

ANALYZE THE RHETORICAL CONTEXT

Communication as Conversation

Notice that in the previous discussion, the fact that Barbara Jordan's "Statement on the Articles of Impeachment" was originally delivered before the House Judiciary Committee did not matter much. Nor did it matter when the speech was published (July 24, 1974), who gave it, who exactly heard the speech, what their reaction was, or what other people were saying at the time. Textual analysis can proceed as if the item under consideration "speaks for all time," as if it is a museum piece unaffected by time and space. There's nothing wrong with museums, of course; they permit people to observe and appreciate objects in an important way. But museums often fail to reproduce an artwork's original context and cultural meaning. In that sense, museums can diminish understanding as much as they contribute to it. Contextual rhetorical analysis is an attempt to understand communications through the lens of their environments, examining the rough-and-tumble, real-world setting or scene out of which any communication emerges.

Contextual analysis, like textual analysis, may be conducted in any number of ways. But contextual rhetorical analysis always proceeds from a description of the **rhetorical situation** that motivated the event in question. It demands an appreciation of the social circumstances that call rhetorical events into being and that orchestrate the course of those events. It regards communications as anything but self-contained. Contextual rhetorical analysis assumes that

- Every communication is a response to other communications and to other social practices—part of an ongoing conversation, not an isolated monologue.

- Communications, and social practices more generally, reflect the attitudes and values of the living communities that sustain them.

- Analysts seek evidence of how those other communications and social practices are reflected in texts.

Rhetorical analysis from a contextualist perspective understands individual pieces as parts of ongoing conversations.

The challenge is to reconstruct the conversation surrounding a specific piece of writing or speaking. Sometimes it is easy to do so. For example, sometimes there are obvious references to the context in the very words of an argument. Or sometimes you may have appropriate background information on the topic, as well as a feel for what is behind what people are writing or saying about it.

But other times it takes some research to reconstruct the conversations and social practices related to a particular issue. If the issue is current, you need to study how the debate is conducted in current blogs, magazines, newspapers, talk shows, movies and TV shows, Web sites, and so forth. If the issue is from an earlier time, you must do archival research into historical collections of newspapers, magazines, books, letters, and other documentary sources in order to develop a feel for the rhetorical situation that generated the argument under analysis.

Let's return now to a discussion of Jordan's "Statement" on pages 33–37. With a bit of research it is possible to reconstruct some of the "conversations" that Jordan is participating in, and the result will be an enhanced understanding of her speech as well as an appreciation for how you might do a contextual rhetorical analysis.

Jordan's Life and Works

You can begin by learning more about Jordan herself. The headnote to the speech on page 33 provides some facts about her (e.g., that she is African American, that she went to law school, that she was elected to the U.S. House of Representatives at the age of just 36; that she came to prominence during the Watergate hearings).

Jordan was a relative unknown when she gave her speech; even her colleagues in Congress did not know her well. She had recently been elected to Congress as a young woman in part because of the support of Lyndon Johnson, a fellow Texan who preceded Richard Nixon as president. Johnson then advocated for her placement on the House Judiciary Committee, chaired by Democrat Peter Rodino of New Jersey; this was a highly prized, prestigious appointment that rarely goes to a freshman congressperson. Thus Jordan came to her speech with a reputation as being beholden to Johnson and the Democratic Party. Her challenge therefore was to avoid the appearance of partisanship—as we will show below, that explains many of her rhetorical choices.

The Context of the Speech

In one sense, the audience of Jordan's speech consisted of the other 34 members of the House Judiciary Committee, gathered together to decide whether or not to recommend impeachment. And yet Jordan was not at all speaking to a closed committee meeting. Her speech was very public.

The Senate Watergate hearings had been televised the summer before Jordan's speech, from May through July of 1973, and millions of Americans had become accustomed to being glued to their sets to watch sensational testimony by a host of witnesses. The 1973 hearings produced charges that President Nixon may well have authorized break-ins at the Democratic campaign headquarters in Washington during the 1972 election season, that he and members of his leadership team covered up their sponsorship of the break-ins, and that the White House was involved in all sorts of other dirty tricks and improprieties.

Americans remained deeply divided about these accusations until it was discovered that Nixon had himself collected possible hard evidence: he had taped many conversations in the Oval Office, tapes that could support or refute the charges against the president. But for the next year, Nixon engaged in a protracted legal battle to keep the tapes from being disclosed, on the grounds that they were private conversations protected under "executive privilege": Nixon and his lawyers argued that the public interest would be undermined if leaders could not keep private conversations private. During that time Nixon's vice president, Spiro Agnew, was forced to resign, and a number of his advisers (including John Dean, H. R. Haldeman, John Ehrlichman, and Attorney General John Mitchell) were indicted and convicted on charges of obstructing justice. Partial and edited transcripts of the tapes were produced sporadically by the president, under pressure, but those produced only further rancor, particularly when 18 minutes of a key conversation were mysteriously erased.

These events created a continuing national uproar and sustained headlines and discussion. The House Judiciary Committee opened hearings into whether the president should be impeached beginning on May 9, 1974. Those closed meetings moved slowly, deliberately, and inconclusively all during the summer of 1974. Finally on July 24, 1974, the courts ruled that Nixon had to turn all his remaining tapes over. That same day, knowing that hard evidence was now at hand, the House Judiciary Committee immediately went into session to vote whether to impeach Nixon. And in keeping with the Senate Watergate hearings, these sessions were open and televised to the nation. Peter Rodino decided to give each member of the committee 15 minutes to make a public opening statement that would be carried on television to the nation. Barbara Jordan was therefore speaking not just to congressional colleagues but to millions of citizens who had never heard of her but who were mightily interested in what she would have to say.

As it turned out, she was scheduled to speak at 9 p.m. on July 24, 1974—prime time. The nation was ready to listen to her argument. And Jordan was ready to deliver: she would call for impeachment, and she would do so in a way that was absolutely principled and nonpartisan.

The Larger Conversation

We could offer much more contextualizing background here. We could cite a host of articles, books, news reports, and TV broadcasts in order to establish the nature of the conversation about impeachment that was raging in the nation from the summer of 1973 until President Nixon finally resigned on August 8, 1974. Such an account would establish a rather simple point: the country was bitterly divided on three related issues.

The first was a question of partisanship. His fellow Republicans naturally gave the benefit of the doubt to President Nixon, and that benefit was quite considerable, given that Nixon had won the 1972 election over George McGovern in a landslide. By contrast, Democrats controlled the Senate and the House of Representatives, and they were aggressive in pursuing a case against the president because they stood to gain politically. But partisanship was not supposed to be an issue in an impeachment. When Andrew Johnson was impeached by the House during 1867–1868 (and narrowly acquitted by the Senate), it was apparent that his impeachment was politically motivated. In subsequent years, it therefore was understood that impeachment should never be partisan, should never be politically motivated but based on "treason, bribery, or high crimes and misdemeanors." In the weeks leading up to July 24, supporters of President Nixon, led by his lawyer James D. St. Clair, constantly charged that his adversaries were motivated by purely political purposes. Representative David Dennis of Indiana spoke explicitly of "a political lynching," Representative Charles Sandman of New Jersey and other Republicans had emphasized partisanship earlier in the day during their own 15-minute presentations, and millions of average citizens also suspected that opponents of Nixon wanted to remove him simply to gain political power. On a practical level, since Nixon could be convicted in the Senate only by a two-thirds majority, it was essential that some Republicans come to support conviction. A purely partisan vote—Democratic vs. Republicans—could not succeed.

Barbara Jordan's task was therefore formidable. She had to take the majority, Democratic position—without seeming to take it *because* she was a Democrat. If you scan issues of *Newsweek, Time, The Washington Post*, or *The New York Times* from the summer of 1974, you will see how frequently the Republicans were claiming that President Nixon was the victim of a "partisan vendetta." It was the strategy of his defense team to do so. By contrast, Democrats needed to get at least a half-dozen Republican members of the House Judiciary Committee to support impeachment if the actual impeachment were to succeed in the Senate.

Jordan consequently adopted a number of tactics to establish her nonpartisanship. She begins by identifying herself as a youthful, junior member of the committee, not a Democratic member, and quickly follows by claiming particular and fervent allegiance to the Constitution, not to any political party. Speaking as a custodian of "the public trust," she quotes the Constitution, its framers, and respected authorities such as Alexander Hamilton, Woodrow Wilson, and James Madison—several of them southerners—and avoids names with a partisan identification. And she consistently and frequently uses the pronoun "we" to refer to the entire committee, Republicans and Democrats alike. In all these ways Jordan sought to address the nation on nonpartisan grounds. (And she must have succeeded: over the next three days, the House Judiciary Committee voted in favor of three articles of impeachment—obstruction of justice, abuse of presidential power, and contempt of Congress.)

The second concern in the nation on July 24, 1974, was about hard evidence. The president's former lawyer, John Dean, had accused Nixon of obstructing justice and conspiring to give hush money to Watergate burglars; Watergate gangster Charles Colson at his sentencing hearing had recently claimed that the president obstructed justice; and many other charges had been raised. But supporting evidence was seen as circumstantial; it all appeared to be the president's word against the word of others. The conversation swirling around Barbara Jordan, therefore, was very much concerned with hard evidence, or a so-called "murder weapon" or "smoking gun." Supporters of the president, including Representatives Trent Lott and Charles Wiggins on the Judiciary Committee, constantly claimed that while the charges against Nixon were serious, they were not corroborated by irrefutable evidence. (This claim was ultimately addressed by the tapes that Nixon had collected: earlier on the very day that Jordan spoke, the Supreme Court in an 8–0 vote demanded that Nixon turn over 64 tapes to investigators, and those tapes provided the damning evidence that finally brought Nixon to resign two weeks later.)

In her speech, Jordan addresses the evidence question explicitly, beginning in paragraph 11: "we were told that the evidence which purports to support the allegations…is thin…[and] insufficient." The paragraphs that follow rehearse hard evidence already established—evidence about the break-ins and other crimes committed by Howard

Hunt as well as payments to Hunt; evidence about the payment of hush money (para. 15); evidence cited in paragraphs 16 and 17, including that "the President has made public announcements and assertions bearing on the Watergate case which...he knew to be false." The emphasis on evidence in Jordan's speech definitely derives from the conversations that she was enmeshed in during July of 1974.

The third national concern that Jordan addressed in her speech had to do with a legal issue, one that as a lawyer Jordan was especially qualified to address: Were the actions of President Nixon serious enough to be "impeachable offenses"? As the evidence of presidential wrongdoing piled up, many Americans could see that Nixon had committed all sorts of transgressions. But were they serious enough to justify impeachment? Everyone agreed that if the president had committed a felony, he should be removed; but what about lesser offenses—how high did a crime have to reach in order to be a "high crime," and what "misdemeanors" justified impeachment? As we have already shown in our textual analysis, Jordan in paragraph 6 defines the circumstances of impeachment by quoting the framers of the Constitution directly, and in paragraph 7 concedes that a president should not be removed for incompetence (i.e., "maladministration"). The following paragraphs indicate that public officials should not be removed for "petty reasons" but only for "the grossest offenses." By agreeing that a president should be removed only for very serious offenses, and by establishing that there was indeed hard evidence of the president's guilt in serious offenses, Jordan summed up for the nation the case for impeachment.

Barbara Jordan's specific contribution to the conversation about impeachment in 1974 could be extended for a long time—indefinitely, in fact. There is no need to belabor the point, however; our purpose has been simply to illustrate that contextual analysis of a piece of rhetoric can enrich our understanding of it.

WRITE A RHETORICAL ANALYSIS

Effective rhetorical analysis, as we have seen, can be textual or contextual in nature. The two approaches to rhetorical analysis are never mutually exclusive. Indeed, many if not most analysts operate between these two extremes; they consider the details of the text, but they also attend to the particulars of context. Textual analysis and contextual analysis inevitably complement each other. Getting at what is at stake in "Statement on the Articles of Impeachment" or any other sophisticated argument takes patience and intelligence, research, and careful analysis.

Try to use elements of both kinds of analysis whenever you want to understand a text or other rhetorical event more completely. Rhetoric is "inside" texts, but it is also "outside" them. Specific rhetorical performances are an irreducible mixture of text and context, and so interpretation and analysis of those performances must account for both as well. Remember, however, the limitations of your analysis. Realize that your analysis will always be somewhat partial and incomplete, ready to be deepened, corrected, modified, and extended by the insights of others. Rhetorical analysis can itself be part of an unending conversation—a way of learning and teaching within a community.

ANALYZE A VISUAL ARGUMENT

We live in a world flooded with images. They pull on us, compete for our attention, push us to do things. But unlike verbal arguments, we rarely think about how they work.

Arguments in written language are visual in one sense: we use our eyes to read the words on the page. But without words, can there be a visual argument? Certainly some visual symbols take on conventional meanings. Signs in airports or other public places, for example, are designed to communicate with speakers of many languages.

Some visual symbols even make explicit claims. A one-way street sign says that drivers should travel only in one direction. But are such signs arguments? Most scholars define an argument as a claim supported by one or more reasons. A one-way sign has a claim: all drivers should go in the same direction. But is there a reason? We all know an unstated reason the sign carries: drivers who go the wrong way violate the law and risk a substantial fine (plus they risk a head-on collision with other drivers).

But other visual arguments cannot be explained this easily—even ones that are intended to make claims. Beginning in 1935, the U.S. Farm Security Administration hired photographers to document the effects of the Great Depression and the drought years on Americans. One of the photographers, Dorothea Lange, shot a series of photographs of homeless and destitute migrant workers in California. Her photographs have become some of the most familiar images of the United States in the 1930s. Lange had an immediate goal—getting the government to build a resettlement camp for the homeless workers. She wrote to her boss in Washington that her images were "loaded with ammunition."

Lange titled one of her images "Eighteen-year-old mother from Oklahoma, now a California migrant." The young woman and child in the photograph are obviously poor, living in a tent. Yet the image doesn't immediately suggest suffering. Lange was a portrait photographer before becoming a documentary photographer, and her experience shows. She takes advantage of the highlighting of the woman's

Eighteen-year-old mother from Oklahoma, now a California migrant. (Dorothea Lange/Library of Congress Prints and Photographs Division, FSA/OWI Collection, [LC-USF34-T01-016270-C])

hair from the sun contrasted with the dark interior of the tent to draw our eyes to the woman's face. The woman doesn't appear to be distressed—just bored. Only later do we notice the dirty face of the child and other details. With another caption—perhaps "Young mother on a camping trip left behind while her husband went for a hike"—we might read the photograph to say something else. And even if we take the image as evidence of poverty, Lange's claim is not evident, just as images of homeless people today do not necessarily make arguments.

BUILD A VISUAL ANALYSIS

It's one thing to construct a visual argument yourself; it's another thing to analyze visual arguments that are made by someone else. Fortunately, analyzing arguments made up of images and graphics is largely a matter of following the same strategies for rhetorical analysis that are outlined earlier in this chapter. When you analyze a visual argument, think about the image itself (textual analysis) as well as its relationship to other images and discourses (contextual analysis). The arguments implied by visual images, like the arguments made through text alone, are carried both by the context and by the image.

Analyzing Context

Consider, for example, the advertisement for Hofstra University. The context for the ad is not difficult to uncover through a bit of research. The ad appeared in 1989 and 1990 when Hofstra, located on Long Island 25 miles from New York City, was celebrating its fiftieth anniversary and hoping to use the occasion to enhance its reputation. At the time, Hofstra enjoyed a good reputation for its professional programs, particularly in education and business (which one-third of the 7500 students were majoring in). However, it was not as highly regarded in the core science and humanities disciplines that are often associated with institutional prestige. Hofstra was well known in the New York metropolitan area—half its students were commuting to school rather than living in dormitories—but it was attracting few students from outside the region, and its campus life was consequently regarded as mediocre. Its student body was generally well prepared, hardworking,

What does it take to be the best?

Determination and hard work, at any age, can lead to being the best.
Hofstra University, just 50 years old, is already among the
top ten percent of American colleges and universities in
almost all academic criteria and resources.

Professionally accredited programs in such major areas as business,
engineering, law, psychology and education.

A library with over 1.1 million volumes *on campus*—a collection
larger than that of 95% of American universities.

Record enrollments with students from 31 states and 59 countries—
with a student-faculty ratio of only 17 to 1.

The largest, most sophisticated non-commercial television facility
in the East. A high technology undergraduate teaching
resource with broadcast-quality production capability.

A ranking in *Barron's Guide to the Most Prestigious Colleges*—one of
only 262 colleges and universities chosen from almost 4,000.

At Hofstra, determination, inspiration and hard work are qualities
our faculty demands in itself and instills in our students.

These qualities are what it takes to be the best. In anything.

HOFSTRA UNIVERSITY
WE TEACH SUCCESS.

50th Anniversary
Hempstead, L.I., New York 11550

Ad for Hofstra University, 1989. (Courtesy of Hofstra University) and capable, but its most outstanding applicants were too often choosing other universities.

Feeling that its performance was exceeding its reputation and that it was capable of attracting a more diverse and talented student body, Hofstra conceived a national ad campaign designed to change the opinions of prospective students and their parents, as well as the general public. It placed the ads—the ad reproduced here is one of a series—in several magazines and newspapers in order to persuade people that Hofstra was outstanding in all fields, not just in the professions, and that the opportunities available to its students were varied and valuable.

Analyzing Visual and Textual Elements

Ads make arguments, and the message of the Hofstra ad is something like this: "Hofstra is a prestigious, high-quality institution that brings out the best in students because of its facilities, its academic reputation, its student body, and the strength of its faculty and academic programs." The text of the Hofstra ad expresses that argument specifically: "The best" and "we teach success" are prominently displayed; the size of the print visually reinforces the message; and the fine print supports the main thesis by mentioning Hofstra's facilities (the large library with "a collection [of volumes] larger than that of 95% of American universities," the "television facility...with broadcast quality production capability"); its reputation (its ranking in *Barron's Guide to the Most Prestigious Colleges* and its "professionally accredited programs"); and its faculty and students. The ad works by offering logical reasoning and evidence for its implied claims, as well as appeals to our most fervently held values. By placing the ad in prestigious publications, Hofstra enhanced its credibility even further.

But exactly how does the photograph of the young girl with the flute support the overall argument? Let's look at the ad itself.

- The photo of the girl is black and white, so that it can be printed easily and inexpensively in newspapers and magazines. But the black and white format also contributes a sense of reality and truthfulness, in the manner of black and white photos or documentary films. (Color images, on the other hand, can imply flashiness or commercialism.)

- The girl is young—about 10 or 12 years of age?—and her readiness for distinguished performance suggests that she is a prodigy, a genius. In other words, she is the kind of person that Hofstra attracts and sustains.

- The girl is dressed up for some kind of musical performance, and the details of her costume imply that the performance is of a high order. Her delicacy and refinement are implied by the posture of her fingers, the highly polished flute that she holds with an upright carriage, and the meticulousness of her tie, shirt, and coat.

- The girl's expression suggests that she is serious, sober, disciplined, but comfortable—the kind of student (and faculty member) that Hofstra features. (The layout and consistent print style used in the ad reinforce that impression: by offering a balanced and harmonious placement of elements and by sticking to the same type style throughout, the ad stands for the values of balance, harmony, consistency, and order.)

- The girl is modest and unpretentious in expression, yet she looks directly at the viewer with supreme self-confidence. Her age suggests innocence, yet her face proclaims ambition; her age and the quasi-masculine costume (note that she wears neither a ring nor earrings) give her a sexual innocence that is in keeping with the scholarly ideal.

Come to Hofstra, the image seems to proclaim, and you will meet people who are sober and graceful, self-disciplined and confident, ambitious without being arrogant. The ad is supporting its thesis with good reasons implied by its central image—good reasons that can be identified with logos and pathos.

Speaking of pathos, what do you make of the fact that the girl is Asian? On one hand, the Asian girl's demeanor reinforces cultural stereotypes. Delicate, small, sober, controlled, even humorless, she embodies characteristics that recall other Asian American icons (particularly women), especially icons of success through discipline and hardwork. On the other hand, the girl speaks to the Asian community. It is as if she is on the verge of saying, "Come and join me at Hofstra, where you too can reach the highest achievement. And read the copy below me to learn more about what Hofstra has to offer." In this way the girl participates in Hofstra's ambition to attract highly qualified, highly motivated, and high-performing minority students—as well as any other high-performing student, regardless of ethnicity or gender, who values hard work, academic distinction, and the postponement of sensual gratification in return for long-term success.

No doubt there are other aspects of the image that work to articulate and to support the complex argument of the ad. There is more to be said about this ad, and you may disagree with some of the points we have offered. But consider this: By 2009, 20 years after this ad and others like it were run, Hofstra's total enrollment had climbed above 12,000, including over 7500 undergraduates. Its admissions were more selective, its student body was far more diverse and less regional in character, its graduation rate had improved, its sports teams had achieved national visibility, it opened a new medical school, and its minority student population had grown. Many factors contributed to the university's advancement, but it seems likely that this ad was one of them.

WRITE A VISUAL ANALYSIS

Like rhetorical analysis, effective visual analysis takes into account the context of the image as well as its visual elements and any surrounding text. First look carefully at the image itself. What visual elements grab your attention first, and how do other details reinforce that impression—what is most important and less important? How do color and style influence impressions? How does the image direct the viewer's eyes and reinforce what is important? What is the relationship between the image and any text that might accompany it? Consider the shapes, colors, and details of the image, as well as how the elements of the image connect with different arguments and audiences.

Then think about context. Try to determine why and when the image was created, who created it, where it appeared, and the target audience. Think about how the context of its creation and publication affected its intended audience. What elements have you seen before? Which elements remind you of other visuals?

BARBARA JORDAN

Statement on the Articles of Impeachment

Barbara Jordan (1936–1996) grew up in Houston and received a law degree from Boston University in 1959. Working on John F. Kennedy's 1960 presidential campaign stirred an interest in politics, and Jordon became the first African American woman elected to the Texas State Senate in 1966. In 1972 she was elected to the United States House of Representatives and thus became the first African American woman from the South ever to serve in Congress. Jordan was appointed to the House Judiciary Committee. Soon she was in the national spotlight when that committee considered articles of impeachment against President Richard Nixon, who had illegally covered up a burglary of Democratic Party headquarters during the 1972 election. When Nixon's criminal acts reached to the Judiciary Committee, Jordan's opening speech on July 24, 1974, set the tone for the debate and established her reputation as a moral beacon for the nation. Nixon resigned as president on August 9, 1974, after the House Judiciary Committee voted in favor of three articles of impeachment and when it was evident that his impeachment would be sustained in a trial before the U. S. Senate.

Thank you, Mr. Chairman.

1   Mr. Chairman, I join my colleague Mr. Rangel in thanking you for giving the junior members of this committee the glorious opportunity of sharing the pain of this inquiry. Mr. Chairman, you are a strong man, and it has not been easy but we have tried as best we can to give you as much assistance as possible.

2   Earlier today, we heard the beginning of the Preamble to the Constitution of the United States: "We, the people." It's a very eloquent beginning. But when that document was completed on the seventeenth of September in 1787, I was not included in that "We, the people." I felt somehow for many years that George Washington and Alexander Hamilton just left me out by mistake. But through the process of amendment, interpretation, and court decision, I have finally been included in "We, the people."

3   Today I am an inquisitor. Any hyperbole would not be fictional and would not overstate the solemnness that I feel right now. My faith in the Constitution is whole; it is complete; it is total. And I am not going to sit here and be an idle spectator to the diminution, the subversion, the destruction, of the Constitution (3).

4   "Who can so properly be the inquisitors for the nation as the representatives of the nation themselves?" "The subjects of its jurisdiction are those offenses which proceed from the misconduct of public men." And that's what we're talking about. In other words, [the jurisdiction comes] from the abuse or violation of some public trust.

5   It is wrong, I suggest, it is a misreading of the Constitution for any member here to assert that for a member to vote for an article of impeachment means that that member must be convinced that the President should be removed from office. The Constitution doesn't say that. The powers relating to impeachment are an essential check in the hands of the body of the legislature against and upon the encroachments of the executive. The division between the two branches of the legislature, the House and the Senate, assigning to the one the right to accuse and to the other the right to judge, the framers of this Constitution were very astute. They did not make the accusers and the judgers the same person.

6   We know the nature of impeachment. We've been talking about it awhile now. It is chiefly designed for the President and his high ministers to somehow be called into account. It is designed to "bridle" the executive if he engages in excesses. "It is designed as a method of national inquest into the conduct of public men." The framers confided in the Congress the power if need be, to remove the President in order to strike a delicate balance between a President swollen with power and grown tyrannical, and preservation of the independence of the executive.

7   The nature of impeachment: a narrowly channeled exception to the separation-of-powers maxim. The Federal Convention of 1787 said that. It limited impeachment to high crimes and misdemeanors and discounted and opposed the term *maladministration*. "It is to be used only for great misdemeanors," so it was said in the North Carolina ratification convention. And in the Virginia ratification convention: "We do not trust our liberty to a particular branch. We need one branch to check the other."

8   "No one need be afraid"—the North Carolina ratification convention—"No one need be afraid that officers who commit oppression will pass with immunity." "Prosecutions of impeachments will seldom fail to agitate the passions of the whole community," said Hamilton in the Federalist Papers, number 65. "We divide into parties more or less friendly or inimical to the accused." I do not mean political parties in that sense.

9   The drawing of political lines goes to the motivation behind impeachment; but impeachment must proceed within the confines of the constitutional term "high crime[s] and misdemeanors." Of the impeachment process, it was Woodrow Wilson who said that "Nothing short of the grossest offenses against the plain law of the land will suffice to give them speed and effectiveness. Indignation so great as to overgrow party interest may secure a conviction; but nothing else can."

10   Common sense would be revolted if we engaged upon this process for petty reasons. Congress has a lot to do: Appropriations, Tax Reform, Health Insurance, Campaign Finance Reform, Housing, Environmental Protection, Energy Sufficiency, Mass Transportation. Pettiness cannot be allowed to stand in the face of such overwhelming problems. So today we are not being petty. We are trying to be big, because the task we have before us is a big one.

11   This morning, in a discussion of the evidence, we were told that the evidence which purports to support the allegations of misuse of the CIA by the President is thin. We're told that that evidence is insufficient. What that recital of the evidence this morning did not include is what the President did know on June the 23rd, 1972 (11).

12   The President did know that it was Republican money, that it was money from the Committee for the Re-Election of the President, which was found in the possession of one of the burglars arrested on June the 17th. What the President did know on the 23rd of June was the prior activities of E. Howard Hunt, which included his participation in the break-in of Daniel Ellsberg's psychiatrist, which included Howard Hunt's participation in the Dita Beard ITT affair, which included Howard Hunt's fabrication of cables designed to discredit the Kennedy Administration.

13   We were further cautioned today that perhaps these proceedings ought to be delayed because certainly there would be new evidence forthcoming from the President of the United States. There has not even been

an obfuscated indication that this committee would receive any additional materials from the President. The committee subpoena is outstanding, and if the President wants to supply that material, the committee sits here. The fact is that on yesterday, the American people waited with great anxiety for eight hours, not knowing whether their President would obey an order of the Supreme Court of the United States.

14   At this point, I would like to juxtapose a few of the impeachment criteria with some of the actions the President has engaged in. Impeachment criteria: James Madison, from the Virginia ratification convention. "If the President be connected in any suspicious manner with any person and there be grounds to believe that he will shelter him, he may be impeached."

15   We have heard time and time again that the evidence reflects the payment to the defendants of money. The President had knowledge that these funds were being paid and these were funds collected for the 1972 presidential campaign. We know that the President met with Mr. Henry Petersen 27 times to discuss matters related to Watergate, and immediately thereafter met with the very persons who were implicated in the information Mr. Petersen was receiving. The words are: "If the President is connected in any suspicious manner with any person and there be grounds to believe that he will shelter that person, he may be impeached."

16   Justice Story: "Impeachment" is attended—"is intended for occasional and extraordinary cases where a superior power acting for the whole people is put into operation to protect their rights and rescue their liberties from violations." We know about the Huston plan. We know about the break-in of the psychiatrist's office. We know that there was absolute complete direction on September 3rd when the President indicated that a surreptitious entry had been made in Dr. Fielding's office, after having met with Mr. Ehrlichman and Mr. Young. "Protect their rights." "Rescue their liberties from violation."

17   The Carolina ratification convention impeachment criteria: those are impeachable "who behave amiss or betray their public trust." Beginning shortly after the Watergate break-in and continuing to the present time, the President has engaged in a series of public statements and actions designed to thwart the lawful investigation by government prosecutors. Moreover, the President has made public announcements and assertions bearing on the Watergate case, which the evidence will show he knew to be false. These

assertions, false assertions, impeachable, those who misbehave. Those who "behave amiss or betray the public trust."

18   James Madison again at the Constitutional Convention: "A President is impeachable if he attempts to subvert the Constitution." The Constitution charges the President with the task of taking care that the laws be faithfully executed, and yet the President has counseled his aides to commit perjury, willfully disregard the secrecy of grand jury proceedings, conceal surreptitious entry, attempt to compromise a federal judge, while publicly displaying his cooperation with the processes of criminal justice. "A President is impeachable if he attempts to subvert the Constitution."

19   If the impeachment provision in the Constitution of the United States will not reach the offenses charged here, then perhaps that 18th-century Constitution should be abandoned to a 20th-century paper shredder (19).

20   Has the President committed offenses, and planned, and directed, and acquiesced in a course of conduct which the Constitution will not tolerate? That's the question. We know that. We know the question. We should now forthwith proceed to answer the question. It is reason, and not passion, which must guide our deliberations, guide our debate, and guide our decision.

21   I yield back the balance of my time, Mr. Chairman.

SAMPLE STUDENT RHETORICAL ANALYSIS

T. Jonathan Jackson

Dr. Netaji

English 1301

9 February 2012

An Argument of Reason and Passion: Barbara Jordan's
"Statement on the Articles of Impeachment"

On May 9, 1974, the U.S. House Judiciary Committee
began an impeachment hearing against President Richard
Nixon for his role in the cover-up of the Watergate scandal.
On July 24, 1974, Congresswoman Barbara Jordan stood
before this committee and delivered an 11-minute speech
known as "Statement on the Articles of Impeachment."
The argument of this speech is that the president should
be impeached because his actions threaten both the
Constitution and the people of the United States. Jordan
states, "It is reason, and not passion, which must guide our
deliberation, guide our debate, and guide our decision."
Subsequently, she uses a strong logical argument that she
supports with appeals to both her credibility and the audience's feelings of patriotism for the Constitution.

The context of Jordan's speech is important for three
reasons. First, the charges against Nixon and his impeachment case were controversial because he was a Republican
president and the committee was mostly Democratic. The
burden was on Jordan to show that the case for impeachment was not a partisan issue. Second, the speech was
televised. Jordan was speaking not only to the committee—
an audience well informed about the topic and mostly in
support of her argument—but also to a television audience

that was not as informed and potentially hostile. Finally, although Jordan was already known in Texas politics, she was new to Congress, and she was a low-ranking member of the committee. Consequently, she had to prove her ethos to both the committee and the wider television audience who did not know her.

At the heart of Jordan's argument is her insistence that the Constitution is important because it protects the rights of the American people. Therefore the Constitution itself should be protected. Thus impeachment is the proper punishment for a president or other leaders who upset the balance of power and act against the Constitution. Using evidence from the North Carolina and Virginia Constitutional Conventions, she shows that impeachment is used only for "great misdemeanors" and that we need the branches of government to check the powers of each other. Her next task is to show what these misdemeanors are and to show that Nixon has committed them. Here she appeals to logic in that she not only explains each misdemeanor in full and matches the president's actions to each one, but she also cites reputable sources such as James Madison, who wrote the Federalist Papers; the South Carolina Ratification Convention; and Justice Joseph Story, who as a justice under Madison was known for his work explaining the states' powers under the Constitution. In addition, she emphasizes each point by starting with a key quotation by one of these figures, such as James Madison: "A President is impeachable if he attempts to subvert the Constitution." Then she describes the president's actions that illustrate this quotation— in this case, he told his associates to commit perjury, to

Jackson 3

hide evidence, and to bribe a judge—and stresses the point
with the same quotation she used earlier: "A President is
impeachable if he attempts to subvert the Constitution."
This repetition of the quotation makes the connection both
clearer and more memorable to the audience.

Jordan shows that she has an extensive knowledge
of the Constitution and of the facts in the impeachment
case, which gains her credibility as someone who can speak
knowledgeably on the subject. She also shows her credibility
as a citizen, as well as an African American woman who
relies on the Constitution and the Constitutional process
for protection. She says that when the Constitution was
completed, "I was not included in that 'We, the People.'
I felt somehow for many years that George Washington and
Alexander Hamilton just left me out by mistake. But through
the process of amendment, interpretation, and court decision
I have finally been included in 'We, the People.'"

Jordan also addresses the concern that the impeachment case is partisan, an allegation that could damage
the credibility of the committee. She recognizes that "the
drawing of political lines goes to the motivation behind
impeachment," but such a large crime should transcend
party lines. She backs this assertion by quoting Woodrow
Wilson, who said, "Indignation so great as to overgrow
party interest may secure a conviction; but nothing else
can." Jordan continues, "Thus, party pettiness cannot, and
will not, stand in the way of the committee member's jobs
as representatives of the nation: We are trying to be *big*,
because the task we have before us is a big one."

Jordan claims that passion should not be a part of
the impeachment proceedings, but she uses her passion

for the Constitution to connect to her audience's emotions and sense of patriotism: "My faith in the Constitution is whole, it is complete, it is total. And I am not going to sit here and be an idle spectator to the diminution, the subversion, the destruction of the Constitution." She stirs her audience's emotions by repeatedly creating the sense that the Constitution is in physical danger of being destroyed. Not only is it in danger of being figuratively destroyed by Nixon's crimes, but also a failure to impeach him could also destroy the document's integrity. She makes this destruction literal when she says, "If the impeachment provisions will not reach the offenses charged here, then perhaps that 18th-century Constitution should be abandoned to a 20th-century paper shredder." This dramatic image encourages the audience to imagine Nixon actually shredding the Constitution as he ordered the shredding of documents that could link him to crimes. In addition, she makes the American people responsible; "we," meaning both the committee and the television audience, might as well be shredding the Constitution to bits if Nixon is not impeached.

Jordan makes a strong case for impeachment by first appealing to logic and then using her passion for the Constitution to connect to her audience's patriotism. Significantly, because this speech was also televised, Jordan also emerged to a national audience as a powerful speaker. Her clear, rhythmic style is both dramatic and easy to follow. Jordan's reputation as a powerful speaker continues to this day, as does the importance of her speeches, such as this one and other keynote addresses she made throughout her career. In particular, this argument for exercising the checks and balances within our government in order to protect

Jackson 5

the Constitution and the American people from possible tyranny is an argument that resonates with events today.

Jackson 6

Works Cited

Jordan, Barbara. "Statement on the Articles of Impeachment." *American Rhetoric: Top 100 Speeches.* American Rhetoric, 25 July 1974. Web. 23 Jan. 2012.

STEPS TO WRITING A RHETORICAL ANALYSIS

Step 1 Select an argument to analyze

Find an argument to analyze—a speech or sermon, an op-ed in a newspaper, an ad in a magazine designed for a particular audience, or a commentary on a talk show.

Examples
- Editorial pages of newspapers (but not letters to the editor unless you can find a long and detailed letter)
- Opinion features in magazines such as *Time, Newsweek,* and *U.S. News & World Report*
- Magazines that take political positions such as *National Review, Mother Jones, New Republic, Nation,* and *Slate*
- Web sites of activist organizations (but not blog or newsgroup postings unless they are long and detailed)

Step 2 Analyze the context

Who is the author?

Through research in the library or on the Web, learn all you can about the author of the argument.

- How does the argument you are analyzing repeat arguments previously made by the author?
- What motivated the author to write? What is the author's purpose for writing this argument?

Who is the audience?

Through research, learn all you can about the place where the argument appeared and the audience.

- Who is the anticipated audience?
- How do the occasion and forum for writing affect the argument?

What is the larger conversation?

Through research, find out what else was being said about the subject of your selection. Track down any references made in the text you are examining.

- When did the argument appear?
- What other concurrent pieces of "cultural conversation" (e.g., TV shows, other articles, speeches, Web sites) does the item you are analyzing respond to or "answer"?

Step 3 Analyze the text

Summarize the argument
- What is the main claim?
- What reasons are given in support of the claim?
- How is the argument organized? What are the components, and why are they presented in that order?

What is the medium and genre?
- What is the medium? A newspaper? a scholarly journal? a Web site?
- What is the genre? An editorial? an essay? a speech? an advertisement? What expectations does the audience have about this genre?

What appeals are used?
- **Analyze the ethos.** How does the writer represent himself or herself? Does the writer have any credentials as an authority on the topic? Do you trust the writer?

- **Analyze the logos.** Where do you find facts and evidence in the argument? What kinds of facts and evidence does the writer present? Direct observation? statistics? interviews? surveys? secondhand sources such as published research? quotations from authorities?
- **Analyze the pathos.** Does the writer attempt to invoke an emotional response? Where do you find appeals to shared values? You are a member of that audience, so what values do you hold in common with the writer? What values do you not hold in common?

How would you characterize the style?
- Is the style formal, informal, satirical, or something else? Is the author using the specialized language of a particular group or subgroup?
- Are any metaphors or other figures of speech used?

Step 4 Write a draft

Introduction
- Describe briefly the argument you are analyzing, including where it was published, how long it is, and who wrote it.
- If the argument is about an issue unfamiliar to your readers, supply the necessary background.

Body
- Analyze the context, following Step 2.
- Analyze the text, following Step 3.

Conclusion
- Do more than simply summarize what you have said. You might, for example, end with an example that typifies the argument.
- You don't have to end by either agreeing or disagreeing with the writer. Your task in this assignment is to analyze the strategies the writer uses.

Step 5 Revise, edit, proofread

For detailed instructions, see Chapter 7.
For a checklist to evaluate your draft, see pages 180–182.

3

Writing an Argument

When your instructor gives you a writing assignment, look closely at what you are asked to do. Assignments typically contain a great deal of information, and you have to sort that information. First, circle all the instructions about the length, the due date, the format, the grading criteria, and anything else about the production and conventions of the assignment. This information is important to you, but it doesn't tell you what the paper is supposed to be about.

Often your assignment will contain key words such as *analyze, define, evaluate,* or *propose* that will assist you in determining what direction to take. *Analyze* can mean several things. Your instructor might want you to analyze a piece of writing or the causes of something (see pages 11–26; pages 88–100). *Define* usually means writing a **definition argument**, in which you argue for a definition based on the criteria you set out (see pages 73–88). *Evaluate* indicates an **evaluation argument**, in which you argue that something is good, bad, the best, or the worst in its class according to the criteria that you set out (see pages 100–106). An assignment that contains the instructions *Take a position in regard to a reading* might lead you to write a **rebuttal argument** (see pages 106–114). *Propose* means that you should identify a particular problem and explain why your solution is the best one (see pages 114–126).

If you remain unclear about the purpose of the assignment after reading it carefully, talk with your instructor.

FIND A TOPIC THAT INTERESTS YOU

If your assignment does not provide a specific topic but instead gives you a wide range of options and you don't know what to write about, look first at the materials for your course: the readings, your lecture notes, and discussion boards. Think about what subjects came up in class discussion.

WHAT IS NOT ARGUABLE

- **Statements of fact.** Most facts can be verified by doing research. But even simple facts can sometimes be argued. For example, Mount Everest is usually acknowledged to be the highest mountain in the world at 29,028 feet above sea level. But if the total height of a mountain from base to summit is the measure, then the volcano Mauna Loa in Hawaii is the highest mountain in the world. Although the top of Mauna Loa is 13,667 feet above sea level, the summit is 31,784 above the ocean floor. Thus the "fact" that Mount Everest is the highest mountain on the earth depends on a definition of *highest*. You could argue for this definition—assuming you can find someone who cares.

- **Claims of personal taste.** Your favorite food and your favorite color are examples of personal taste. If you hate fresh tomatoes, no one can convince you that you actually like them. But many claims of personal taste turn out to be value judgments using arguable criteria. For example, if you think that *Alien* is the best science-fiction movie ever made, you can argue that claim using evaluative criteria that other people can consider as good reasons. Indeed, you might not even like science fiction and still argue that *Alien* is the best science-fiction movie ever.

- **Statements of belief or faith.** If someone accepts a claim as a matter of religious belief, then for that person, the claim is true and cannot be refuted. Of course, people still make arguments about the existence of God and which religion reflects the will of God. Whenever an audience will not consider an idea, it's possible but very difficult to construct an argument. Many people claim to have evidence that UFOs exist, but most people refuse to acknowledge that evidence as even being possibly factual.

If you need to look outside class for a topic, think about what interests you. Subjects we argue about often find us. There are enough of them in daily life. We're late for work or class because the traffic is heavy or the bus doesn't run on time. We can't find a place to park when we get to school or work. We have to negotiate through various bureaucracies for almost anything we do—making an appointment to see a doctor, getting a course added or dropped, or correcting a mistake on a bill. Most of the time we grumble and let it go at that. But sometimes we stick with a subject and come up with a solution. Neighborhood groups in cities and towns have been especially effective in getting something done by writing about it—for example, stopping a new road from being built, getting better police and fire protection, and getting a vacant lot turned into a park.

If you are still stuck for an idea, consider writing about the issues that are engaging others in your community. Is there an issue on campus that people are riled up about? Is your local city council or school board debating a topic that is engaging the community? Are two of your friends always at odds on certain issues? Then you might want to enter into those debates yourself. Even if those issues aren't especially compelling to you individually, you will find yourself learning plenty in the course of entering the conversation.

List and Analyze Issues

A good way to get started is to list possible issues to write about. Make a list of questions that can be answered "YES, because..." or "NO, because...." (Check the following lists for some suggestions to get you started.) Think about issues that affect your campus, your community, the nation, and the world. Which issues interest you? About which issues could you make a contribution to the larger discussion?

Campus
✔ Should smoking be banned on campus?
✔ Should varsity athletes get paid for playing sports that bring in revenue?
✔ Should admissions decisions be based exclusively on academic achievement?

✔ Should knowledge of a foreign language be required for all degree plans?

✔ Is there any way to curb the dangerous drinking habits of many students on your campus?

Community

✔ Should people who ride bicycles and motorcycles be required to wear helmets?

✔ Should high schools be allowed to search students for drugs at any time?

✔ Should bilingual education programs be eliminated?

✔ Should bike lanes be built throughout your community to encourage more people to ride bicycles?

✔ Should more tax dollars be shifted from building highways to funding public transportation?

Nation/World

✔ Should driving while talking on a cell phone be banned?

✔ Should capital punishment be abolished?

✔ Should the Internet be censored?

✔ Should beef and poultry be free of growth hormones?

✔ Should people who are terminally ill be allowed to end their lives?

Narrowing a list

1. Put a check beside the issues that look most interesting to write about or the ones that mean the most to you.

2. Put a question mark beside the issues that you don't know very much about. If you choose one of these issues, you will probably have to do in-depth research—by talking to people, by using the Internet, or by going to the library.

3. Select the two or three issues that look most promising. For each issue, make another list:

   • Who is most interested in this issue?

   • Whom or what does this issue affect?

- What are the pros and cons of this issue? Make two columns. At the top of the left one, write "YES, because." At the top of the right one, write "NO, because."

- What has been written about this issue? How can you find out what has been written?

Find a Topic on the Web

Online subject directories can help you identify the subtopics of a large, general topic. Try the subject index of your library's online catalog. You'll likely find subtopics listed under large topics. Also, your library's Web site may have a link to the *Opposing Viewpoints* database.

One of the best Web subject directories for finding arguments is Yahoo's Issues and Causes directory (dir.yahoo.com/Society_and_Culture/Issues_and_Causes/). This directory provides subtopics for major issues and provides links to the Web sites of organizations interested in particular issues.

EXPLORE YOUR TOPIC

When you identify a potential topic, make a quick exploration of that topic, much as you would walk through a house or an apartment you are thinking about renting for a quick look. One way of exploring is to visualize the topic by making a map.

If you live in a state on the coast that has a high potential for wind energy, you might argue that your state should provide financial incentives for generating more electricity from the wind. Perhaps it seems like a no-brainer to you because wind power consumes no fuel and causes no air pollution. The only energy required is for the manufacture and transportation of the wind turbines and transmission lines. But your state and other coastal states may not have exploited potential wind energy for three reasons:

1. **Aesthetics.** Some people think wind turbines are ugly, akin to power lines.

2. **Hazard to wildlife.** A few poorly located wind turbines have killed birds and bats.

3. **Cost.** Wind power costs differ, but wind energy is generally more expensive than electricity produced by burning coal.

To convince other people that your proposal is a good one, you will have to answer these objections.

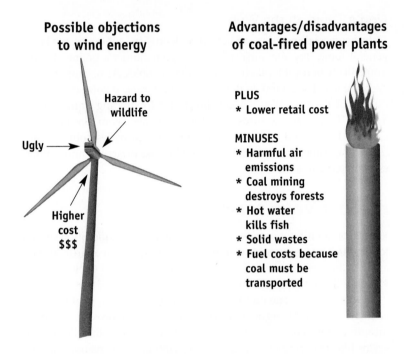

**Possible objections
to wind energy**

Ugly

Hazard to
wildlife

Higher
cost
$$$

**Advantages/disadvantages
of coal-fired power plants**

PLUS
* Lower retail cost

MINUSES
* Harmful air
emissions
* Coal mining
destroys forests
* Hot water
kills fish
* Solid wastes
* Fuel costs because
coal must be
transported

The first two objections are relatively easy to address. Locating wind farms ten kilometers offshore keeps them out of sight and away from most migrating birds and all bats. The third objection, higher cost, is more difficult. One strategy is to argue that the overall costs of wind energy and energy produced by burning coal are comparable if environmental costs are included. You can analyze the advantages and disadvantages of each by drawing maps.

These maps can help you organize an argument for providing financial incentives for wind energy.

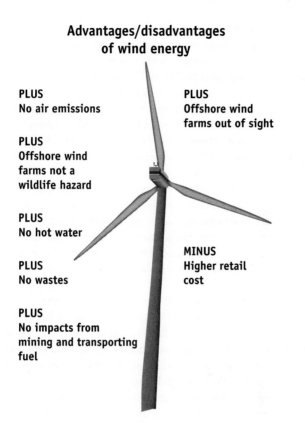

Advantages/disadvantages of wind energy

PLUS
No air emissions

PLUS
Offshore wind
farms not a
wildlife hazard

PLUS
No hot water

PLUS
No wastes

PLUS
No impacts from
mining and transporting
fuel

PLUS
Offshore wind
farms out of sight

MINUS
Higher retail
cost

READ ABOUT YOUR TOPIC

Much college writing draws on and responds to sources—books, articles, reports, and other material written by other people. Every significant issue discussed in today's world has an extensive history of discussion involving many people and various points of view. Before you formulate a claim about a significant issue, you need to become familiar with the conversation that's in progress by reading about it.

One of the most controversial and talked-about subjects in recent years is the outsourcing of white-collar and manufacturing jobs to low-wage nations. Since 2000 an estimated 400,000 to 500,000 American jobs each year have gone to cheap overseas labor markets. The Internet has made this migration of jobs possible, allowing companies to outsource not only low-skilled jobs but also highly skilled jobs in fields such as software development, data storage, and even examining X-rays and MRI scans.

You may have read about this or another complex and controversial topic in one of your courses. Just as in a conversation with several people who hold different views, you may agree with some people, disagree with some, and with others agree with some of their ideas up to a point but then disagree.

CNN commentator Lou Dobbs has been sharply critical of outsourcing. In *Exporting America: Why Corporate Greed Is Shipping American Jobs Overseas* (2006), Dobbs blames large corporations for putting profits ahead of the good of the nation. He accuses both Republicans and Democrats of ignoring the effects of a massive trade deficit and the largest national debt in American history, which Dobbs claims will eventually destroy the American way of life.

Thomas Friedman, columnist for *The New York Times*, takes a different viewpoint on outsourcing in *The World Is Flat: A Brief History of the Twenty-first Century* (2006). By *flat*, Friedman means that the nations of the world are connected like never before through the Internet and the lowering of trade barriers, putting every nation in direct competition with all the others. Friedman believes that outsourcing is not only unstoppable but also desirable. He argues that Americans need to adapt to the new reality and rethink our system of education, or else we will be left hopelessly uncompetitive.

If you decide to write an argument about the issue of outsourcing, you might use either Dobbs's or Friedman's book as your starting point in making a claim. You could begin by using either book to disagree, to agree, or to agree up to a point and then disagree.

No: Disagreeing with a Source

It's easy to disagree by simply saying an idea is dumb, but readers expect you to be persuasive about why you disagree and to offer reasons to support your views.

> X claims that _____, but this view is mistaken because _____.

Example claim: Arguing against outsourcing resulting from free-trade policies
Thomas Friedman claims that the world is "flat," giving a sense of a level-playing field for all, but it is absurd to think that the millions of starving children in the world have opportunities similar to those in affluent countries who pay $100 for basketball shoes made by the starving children.

Example claim: Arguing in favor of outsourcing resulting from free-trade policies
Lou Dobbs is a patriotic American who recognizes the suffering of manufacturing workers in industries like steel and automobiles, but he neglects to realize that the major cause of the loss of manufacturing jobs in the United States and China alike is increased productivity—the 40 hours of labor necessary to produce a car just a few years ago has now been reduced to 15.

Yes: Agreeing with a Source with an Additional Point

Sources should not make your argument for you. With sources that support your position, indicate exactly how they fit into your argument with an additional point.

> I agree with _____ and will make the additional point that _____.

Example claim: Arguing against outsourcing resulting from free-trade policies
Lou Dobbs's outcry against the outsourcing of American jobs also has a related argument: We are dependent not only on foreign oil but also foreign clothing, foreign electronics, foreign tools, foreign toys, and foreign cars and trucks—indeed, just about everything—which is quickly eroding the world leadership of the United States.

Example claim: Arguing in favor of outsourcing resulting from free-trade policies
Thomas Friedman's claim that the Internet enables everyone to become an entrepreneur is demonstrated by thousands of Americans, including my aunt, who could retire early because she developed an income stream by buying jeans and children's clothes at garage sales and selling them to people around the world on eBay.

Yes, But: Agreeing and Disagreeing Simultaneously with a Source

Incorporating sources is not a matter of simply agreeing or disagreeing with them. Often you will agree with a source up to a point, but you will come to a different conclusion. Or you may agree with the conclusions, but not agree with the reasons put forth.

> **I agree with _____ up to a point, but I disagree with the conclusion _____ because _____.**

Example claim: Qualifying the argument against outsourcing resulting from free-trade policies
Lou Dobbs accurately blames our government for giving multinational corporations tax breaks for exporting jobs rather than regulating the loss of millions of jobs, but the real problem lies in the enormous appetite of Americans for inexpensive consumer products like HD televisions, an appetite that is supported by borrowing money from overseas to the point that our dollar has plummeted in value.

Example claim: Qualifying the argument in favor of outsourcing resulting from free-trade policies
Thomas Friedman's central claim that the world is being "flattened" by globalization and there is not much we can do to stop it is essentially correct, but he neglects the social costs of globalization around the world, where the banner of free trade has been the justification for devastating the environment, destroying workers' rights and the rights of indigenous peoples, and even undermining the laws passed by representative governments.

RECOGNIZE FALLACIES

Recognizing where arguments go off track is one of the most important aspects of critical reading. What passes as political discourse is often filled with claims that lack evidence or substitute emotions for evidence. Such faulty reasoning often contains one or more **logical fallacies.** For example, politicians know that the public is outraged when the price of gasoline goes up, and they try to score political points by accusing oil companies of price gouging. It sounds good to angry voters—and it may well be true—but unless the politician defines what *price gouging* means and provides evidence that oil companies are guilty, the argument has no more validity than children calling each other bad names on the playground.

Fallacies of logic

* **Begging the question** *Politicians are inherently dishonest because no honest person would run for public office.* The fallacy of begging the question occurs when the claim is restated and passed off as evidence.

* **Either-or** *Either we eliminate the regulation of businesses or else profits will suffer.* The either-or fallacy suggests that there are only two choices in a complex situation. Rarely, if ever, is this the case.

* **False analogies** *Japan quit fighting in 1945 when we dropped nuclear bombs on them. We should use nuclear weapons against other countries.* Analogies always depend on the degree of resemblance of one situation to another. In this case, the analogy fails to recognize that circumstances today are very different from those in 1945. Many countries now possess nuclear weapons, and we know their use could harm the entire world.

* **Hasty generalization** *We have been in a drought for three years; that's a sure sign of climate change.* A hasty generalization is a broad claim made on the basis of a few occurrences. Climate cycles occur regularly over spans of a few years. Climate trends, however, must be observed over centuries.

(Continued on next page)

- **Non sequitur** *A university that can raise a billion dollars from alumni should not have to raise tuition.* A non sequitur (a Latin term meaning "it does not follow") ties together two unrelated ideas. In this case, the argument fails to recognize that the money for capital campaigns is often donated for special purposes such as athletic facilities or scholarships and is not part of a university's general revenue.

- **Oversimplification** *No one would run stop signs if we had a mandatory death penalty for doing it.* This claim may be true, but the argument would be unacceptable to most citizens. More complex, if less definitive, solutions are called for.

- **Post hoc fallacy** *The stock market goes down when the AFC wins the Super Bowl in even years.* The *post hoc* fallacy (from the Latin *post hoc ergo propter hoc,* which means "after this, therefore because of this") assumes that events that follow in time have a causal relationship.

- **Rationalization** *I could have finished my paper on time if my printer had been working.* People frequently come up with excuses and weak explanations for their own and others' behavior. These excuses often avoid actual causes.

- **Slippery slope** *We shouldn't grant citizenship to illegal immigrants now living in the United States because then no one will want to obey our laws.* The slippery slope fallacy maintains that one thing inevitably will cause something else to happen.

Fallacies of emotion and language

- **Bandwagon appeals** *It doesn't matter if I copy a paper off the Web because everyone else does.* This argument suggests that everyone is doing it, so why shouldn't you? But on close examination, it may be that everyone really isn't doing it—and in any case, it may not be the right thing to do.

- **Name-calling** Name-calling is frequent in politics and among competing groups. People level accusations using names such as *radical,*

> *tax-and-spend liberal, racist, fascist, right-wing ideologue.* Unless these terms are carefully defined, they are meaningless.
>
> - **Polarization** *Feminists are all man haters.* Like name-calling, polarization exaggerates positions and groups by representing them as extreme and divisive.
>
> - **Straw man** *Environmentalists won't be satisfied until not a single human being is allowed to enter a national park.* A straw man argument is a diversionary tactic that sets up another's position in a way that can be easily rejected. In fact, only a small percentage of environmentalists would make an argument even close to this one.

FIND GOOD REASONS

Get in the habit of asking the following questions every time you are asked to write an argument.

Can You Argue by Definition?

Probably the most powerful kind of good reason is an **argument from definition**. You can think of a definition as a simple statement: _____ *is a* _____. You use these statements all the time. When you need a course to fulfill your social-science requirement, you look at the list of courses that are defined as social-science courses. You find out that the anthropology class you want to take is one of them. It's just as important when _____ *is not a* _____. Suppose you are taking College Algebra, which is a math course taught by the math department, yet it doesn't count for the math requirement. The reason it doesn't count is because College Algebra is not defined as a college-level math class. So you have to enroll next semester in Calculus I.

Many definitions are not nearly as clear-cut as the math requirement. If you want to argue that cheerleaders are athletes, you will need to define what an athlete is. You start thinking. An athlete competes in an activity, but that definition alone is too broad, since many competitions do not require physical activity. Thus, an athlete must participate in a competitive physical activity and must train for it. But that definition is still not quite narrow enough, since soldiers train for competitive physical activity. You decide to add that the activity must be a sport and that it must require special competence and precision: *Cheerleaders are athletes because true athletes train for and compete in physical sporting events that require special competence and precision.*

If you can get your audience to accept your definitions, you've gone a long way toward convincing them of the validity of your claim. That is why the most controversial issues in our culture—affirmative action, gay rights, pornography, women's rights, privacy rights, gun control, the death penalty—are argued from definition. Is pornography protected by the First Amendment, or is it a violation of women's rights? Is the death penalty just or cruel and inhumane? You can see from these examples that definitions often rely on deeply held beliefs.

Because people have strong beliefs about controversial issues, they often don't care about the practical consequences. Arguing that it is much cheaper to execute prisoners who have been convicted of first-degree murder than to keep them in prison for life does not convince those who believe that it is morally wrong to kill. (See pages 73–88.)

Can You Argue from Value?

A special kind of argument from definition, one that often implies consequences, is the **argument from value**. You can support your claim with a "because" clause (or several of them) that includes a sense of evaluation. Arguments from value follow from claims like _____ *is a good* _____, or _____ *is not a good* _____.

Evaluation arguments usually proceed from the presentation of certain criteria. These criteria come from the definitions of good and bad, of poor and not so poor, that prevail in a given case. A great burger fulfills certain criteria; so does an outstanding movie, an excellent class, or the best laptop in your price range. Sometimes the criteria are straightforward, as in the burger example. A great burger has to have tasty meat—tender and without gristle, fresh, never frozen—a fresh bun that is the right size, and your favorite condiments. But if you are buying a laptop computer and want to play the latest games along with your school tasks, you need to do some homework. For realistic graphics the best laptop will have a fast processor, a long-lasting battery, connectivity to your wireless accessories, and sturdy construction. The keys for evaluation arguments are finding the appropriate criteria and convincing your readers that those criteria are the right criteria (see pages 100–106).

Can You Argue from Consequence?

Another powerful source of good reasons comes from considering the possible consequences of your position: Can you sketch out the good things that will follow from your position? Can you establish that certain bad things will be avoided if your position is adopted? If so, you will have other good reasons to use.

Causal arguments take the basic form of _____ *causes* _____ (or _____ *does not cause* _____). Very often, causal arguments are more complicated, taking the form _____ *causes* _____ *which, in turn, causes* _____ and so on. The pesticide DDT was banned in the United States as the result of an effective causal argument set out in Rachel Carson's *Silent Spring,* which makes powerful arguments from consequence. The key to Carson's argument is the causal chain that explains how animals and people are poisoned. Carson describes how nothing exists alone in nature. When a potato field is sprayed with DDT, some of that poison is absorbed by the skin of the potatoes and some washes into the groundwater, where it contaminates drinking water. Other poisonous residue is absorbed into streams, where it is ingested by insect larvae, which in turn are eaten by fish. Fish are eaten by other fish, which are then eaten by waterfowl and people. At each stage, the poisons become more concentrated. (See pages 88–100.)

Proposal arguments are future-oriented arguments from consequence. In a proposal argument, you cannot stop with naming good reasons; you also have to show that these consequences would follow from the idea or course of action that you are arguing. For example, if you are proposing designated lanes for bicycles on the streets of your city, you must argue that they will encourage more people to ride bicycles to work and school, reducing air pollution and traffic congestion for everyone. (See pages 114–126.)

Can You Counter Objections to Your Position?

Another good way to find convincing good reasons is to think about possible objections to your position. If you can imagine how your audience might counter or respond to your argument, you will probably include in your argument precisely the points that will address your readers' particular needs and objections. If you are successful, your readers will be convinced that you are right. You've no doubt had the experience of mentally saying to a writer in the course of your reading, "Yeah, but what about this other idea?"—only to have the writer address precisely this objection.

You can impress your readers if you've thought about why anyone would oppose your position and exactly how that opposition would be expressed. If you are writing a proposal argument for a computer literacy requirement for all high school graduates, you might think about why anyone would object, since computers are becoming increasingly important to our jobs and lives. What will the practical objections be? What about philosophical ones? Why hasn't such a requirement been put in place already? By asking such questions in your own arguments, you are likely to develop convincing reasons.

Sometimes, writers pose rhetorical questions such as, "You might say, 'But won't paying for computers for all students make my taxes go up?'" Stating objections explicitly can be effective if you make the objections as those of a reasonable person with an alternative point of view. But if the objections you state are ridiculous or contrived, then you risk being accused of setting up a **straw man**—that is, making the position opposing your own so simplistic that no one would likely identify with it. (See pages 106–114.)

FIND EVIDENCE TO SUPPORT GOOD REASONS

Good reasons are essential ingredients of good arguments, but they don't do the job alone. You must support or verify good reasons with evidence. **Evidence** consists of hard data, examples, personal experiences, episodes, or tabulations of episodes (known as **statistics**) that are seen as relevant to the good reasons you are putting forward. Thus, a writer of arguments puts forward not only claims and good reasons but also evidence that those good reasons are true.

How much supporting evidence should you supply? How much evidence is enough? As is usual in the case of rhetoric, the best answer is, "It depends." If a reader is likely to find one of your good reasons hard to believe, then you should be aggressive in offering support. You should present detailed evidence in a patient and painstaking way. As one presenting an argument, you have a responsibility not just to *state* a case but to *make* a case with evidence. Arguments that are unsuccessful tend to fail not because of a shortage of good reasons; more often, they fail because the reader doesn't agree that there is enough evidence to support the good reason that is being presented.

When a writer doesn't provide satisfactory evidence to support a reason, readers might feel that there has been a failure in the reasoning process. In fact, earlier in this chapter you learned about various **fallacies** associated with faulty arguments (see pages 55–57). But strictly speaking, there is nothing false about these so-called logical fallacies. The fallacies most often refer to failures in providing evidence; when you don't provide enough good evidence to convince your audience, you might be accused of committing a fallacy in reasoning. You will usually avoid such accusations if the evidence that you cite is both *relevant* and *sufficient*.

Relevance refers to the appropriateness of the evidence to the case at hand. Some kinds of evidence are seen as more relevant than others for particular audiences. On the one hand, in science and industry, personal testimony is seen as having limited relevance, while experimental procedures and controlled observations have far more credibility. Compare someone who defends the use of a particular piece of computer software because "it worked for me" with someone who defends it because "according to a journal article published last month, 84 percent of the users of the software were satisfied or very satisfied with it." On the other hand, in writing to the general public on controversial issues such as gun control, personal experience is often considered more relevant than other kinds of data.

Sufficiency refers to the amount of evidence cited. Sometimes a single piece of evidence or a single instance will carry the day if it is especially compelling in some way—if it represents the situation well or makes a point that isn't particularly controversial. More often, people expect more than one piece of evidence if they are to be convinced of something. Convincing readers that they should approve a state-wide computer literacy requirement for all high school graduates will require much more evidence than the story of a single graduate who succeeded with her computer skills. You will likely need statistical evidence for such a broad proposal.

If you anticipate that your audience might not accept your evidence, face the situation squarely. First, think carefully about the argument you are presenting. If you cannot cite adequate evidence for your assertions, perhaps those assertions must be modified or qualified in some way. If you remain convinced of your assertions, then think about doing more research to come up with additional evidence.

STATE AND EVALUATE YOUR THESIS

Once you have identified a topic and have a good sense of how to develop it, the next critical step is to write a **working thesis**. Your **thesis** states your main claim. Much writing that you will do in college and later in your career will require an explicit thesis, usually placed near the beginning.

Focus Your Thesis

The thesis can make or break your paper. If the thesis is too broad, you cannot do justice to the argument. Who wouldn't wish for fewer traffic accidents, better medical care, more effective schools, or a cleaner environment? Simple solutions for these complex problems are unlikely.

Stating something that is obvious to everyone isn't an arguable thesis. Don't settle for easy answers. When a topic is too broad, a predictable thesis often results. Narrow your focus and concentrate on the areas where you have the most questions. Those are likely the areas where your readers will have the most questions too.

The opposite problem is less common: a thesis that is too narrow. If your thesis simply states a commonly known fact, then it is too narrow. For example, the growth rate of the population in the United States has doubled since 1970 because of increased immigration. The U.S. Census Bureau provides reasonably accurate statistical information, so this claim is not arguable. But the policies that allow increased immigration and the effects of a larger population—more crowding and higher costs of health care, education, and transportation—are arguable.

Not arguable: The population of the United States grew faster in the 1990s than in any previous decade because Congress increased the rate of legal immigration and the government stopped enforcing most laws against illegal immigration in the interior of the country.

Arguable: Allowing a high rate of immigration helps the United States deal with the problems of an increasingly aging society and helps provide funding for millions of Social Security recipients.

Arguable: The increase in the number of visas to foreign workers in technology industries is a major cause of unemployment for U. S. citizens in those industries.

Evaluate Your Thesis

Once you have a working thesis, ask these questions:

- Is it arguable?
- Is it specific?
- Is it manageable given your length and time requirements?
- Is it interesting to your intended readers?

Example 1

Sample thesis. We should take action to resolve the serious traffic problem in our city.

Is it arguable? The thesis is arguable, but it lacks a focus.

Is it specific? The thesis is too broad.

Is it manageable? Transportation is a complex issue. New highways and rail systems are expensive and take many years to build. Furthermore, citizens don't want new roads running through their neighborhoods.

Is it interesting? The topic has the potential to be interesting if the writer can propose a specific solution to a problem that everyone in the city recognizes.

When a thesis is too broad, it needs to be revised to address a specific aspect of an issue. Make the big topic smaller.

> **Revised thesis.** The existing freight railway that runs through the center of the city should be converted to a passenger railway because this is the cheapest and quickest way to decrease traffic congestion downtown.

Example 2

> **Sample thesis.** Over 60 percent of Americans play computer games on a regular basis.

Is it arguable? The thesis states a commonly acknowledged fact. It is not arguable.

Is it specific? The thesis is too narrow.

Is it manageable? A known fact is stated in the thesis, so there is little to research. Several surveys report this finding.

Is it interesting? The popularity of computer games is well established. Nearly everyone is aware of the trend.

There's nothing original or interesting about stating that Americans love computer games. Think about what is controversial. One debatable topic is how computer games affect children.

> **Revised thesis.** Computer games are valuable because they improve children's visual attention skills, literacy skills, and computer literacy skills.

THINK ABOUT YOUR READERS

Thinking about your readers doesn't mean telling them what they might want to hear. Instead, imagine yourself in a dialogue with your readers. What questions will they likely have? How might you address any potential objections?

Think About What Your Readers Know—and Do Not Know

Your readers' knowledge of your subject is critical to the success of your argument. If they are not familiar with the background information, they probably won't understand your argument fully. If you know that your readers will be unfamiliar with your subject, you have to supply background information before attempting to convince them of your position. A good tactic is to tie your new information to what your readers already know. Comparisons and analogies can be very helpful in linking old and new information.

Think About Your Readers' Attitudes Toward You

Readers trust writers who know what they are talking about and take a balanced view. Readers respect writers who have done their homework and represent opposing viewpoints fairly. Readers also respect writers who write well. Nothing undermines your credibility faster than numerous errors and sloppy sentences.

Think About Your Readers' Attitudes Toward Your Subject

People have prior attitudes about controversial issues. You must take these attitudes into consideration as you write or speak. Imagine, for instance, that you are preparing an argument for a guest editorial in your college newspaper. You are advocating that your state government should provide parents with choices between public and private schools. You plan to argue that the tax dollars that now automatically go to public schools should go to private schools if parents so choose. You have evidence that the sophomore-to-senior dropout rate in private schools is less than half the rate in public schools. Furthermore, students from private schools attend college at nearly twice the rate of public-school graduates. You intend to argue that one of the reasons private schools are more successful is that they spend more money on instruction and less on administration. And you believe that school choice speaks to the American desire for personal freedom.

Not everyone on your campus will agree with your position. How might the faculty at your college or university feel about this issue? How about the administrators, the staff, other students, and interested community members who read the student newspaper? What are their attitudes toward public funding of private schools? How are you going to deal with the objection that many students in private schools do better in school because they come from more affluent families? And what will the faculty think about you? Will they think you have enough expertise to sound off reliably on the topic? How will you have to buttress your credibility?

Even when you write about a much less controversial subject, you must think carefully about your audience's attitudes toward what you have to say or to write. Sometimes your audience may share your attitudes; other times, your audience may be neutral. At still other times, your audience will have attitudes that differ sharply from your own. Anticipate these various attitudes and act accordingly. If these attitudes are different from yours, you will have to work hard to counter them without insulting your audience.

ORGANIZE YOUR ARGUMENT

Asking a series of questions can generate a list of good reasons, but even if you have plenty, you still have to decide which ones to use and in what order to present them. Thinking about your readers' knowledge, attitudes, and values will help you to decide which reasons to present to your audience.

Writing plans often take the form of outlines, either formal outlines or working outlines. A **formal outline** typically begins with the thesis statement, which anchors the entire outline.

MANAGING THE RISKS OF NANOTECHNOLOGY
WHILE REAPING THE REWARDS

THESIS: The revolutionary potential of nanotechnology has arrived in an explosion of consumer products, yet our federal government has yet to recognize the potential risks or to fund research to reduce those risks.

I. Nanotechnology now is in many consumer products.

  A. The promise of nanotechnology to revolutionize medicine, energy production, and communication is years in the future, but consumer products are here now.

  B. Nanotechnology is now in clothing, food, sports equipment, medicines, electronics, and cars.

  C. Experts predict that 15 percent of manufactured products worldwide will contain nanotechnology in 2014.

  D. The question that hasn't been asked: Is nanotechnology safe?

II. Americans have little awareness of nanotechnology.

  A. Companies have stopped mentioning and advertising nanotechnology.

  B. Companies and the insurance industry paid $250 billion in asbestos claims in the United States alone.

  C. Companies fear exposure to lawsuits if nanotechnology is found to be toxic.

A **working outline** is a sketch of how you will arrange the major sections.

MANAGING THE RISKS OF NANOTECHNOLOGY
WHILE REAPING THE REWARDS

SECTION 1: Begin by defining nanotechnology—manipulating particles between 1 and 100 nanometers (nanometer is a billionth of a meter). Describe the rapid spread of nanotechnology in consumer products including clothing, food, sports equipment, medicines, electronics, and cars. State projection of 15 percent of global manufactured goods containing nanotechnology in 2014.

SECTION 2: Most Americans know nothing about nanotechnology. Companies have stopped advertising that their products contain nanotechnology because of fear of potential lawsuits. Asbestos, once thought safe, now is known to be toxic and has cost companies $250 billion in lawsuits in the United States alone.

SECTION 3: Almost no research has been done on the safety of nanotechnology, only $11 million in federal research. No testing is required for new products because the materials are common, but materials behave differently at nano-scale (e.g., aluminum is normally inert but combustible at nano-scale).

SECTION 4: Nanoparticles are highly mobile and can cross the blood-brain barrier and through the placenta. They are toxic in brains of fish and may collect in lungs.

SECTION 5: Urge that the federal government develop a master plan for identifying and reducing potential risks of nanotechnology and provide sufficient funding to carry out the plan.

WRITE AN ENGAGING TITLE AND INTRODUCTION

Many writers don't think much about titles, but they are very important. A good title makes the reader want to see what you have to say. Be specific as you can in your title, and if possible, suggest your stance.

Get off to a fast start in your introduction. Convince your reader to keep reading. Cut to the chase. Think about how you can get your readers interested. Consider using one of the following.

- a concisely stated thesis
- a hard-hitting fact
- a question
- a vivid description of a problem
- a contradiction or paradox
- a scenario

MANAGING THE RISKS OF NANOTECHNOLOGY
WHILE REAPING THE REWARDS

The revolutionary potential of nanotechnology for medicine, energy production, and communication is now at the research and development stage, but the future has arrived in consumer products. Nanotechnology has given us products we hardly could have imagined just a few years ago: socks that never stink; pants that repel water yet keep you cool; eyeglasses that won't scratch; "smart" foods that add nutrition and reduce cholesterol; DVDs that are incredibly lifelike; bandages that speed healing; tennis balls that last longer; golf balls that fly straighter; pharmaceuticals that selectively deliver drugs; various digital devices like iPads, digital cameras, and smart phones that have longer battery lives and more vivid displays; and cars that are lighter, stronger, and more fuel efficient. These miracle products are now possible because scientists have learned how to manipulate nano-scale particles of 1–100 nanometers (a nanometer is a billionth of a meter; a human hair is about 100,000 nanometers in width). Experts estimate that 15 percent of all consumer products will contain nanotechnology by 2014. In the rush to create new consumer products, however, one question has not been asked: Is nanotechnology safe for those who use the products and the workers who are exposed to nanoparticles daily?

WRITE A STRONG CONCLUSION

Restating your thesis usually isn't the best way to finish a paper. Conclusions that offer only a summary bore readers. The worst endings say something like "in my paper I've said this." Effective conclusions are interesting and provocative, leaving readers with something to think about. Give your readers something to take away besides a straight summary; if you must offer a summary, at least offer it in a new and memorable way. Instead of summarizing, try one of these approaches.

- Issue a call to action.
- Discuss the implications.
- Make recommendations.
- Project into the future.
- Tell an anecdote that illustrates a key point.

The potential risks of nanotechnology are reasonably well known. Among the more obvious research questions are the following:

- How hazardous are nanoparticles for workers who have daily exposure?
- What happens to nanoparticles when they are poured down the drain and eventually enter streams, lakes, and oceans?
- How readily do nanoparticles penetrate the skin?
- What happens when nanoparticles enter the brain?
- What effect do airborne nanoparticles have on the lungs?

Nanotechnology promises untold benefits beyond consumer goods in the fields of medicine, energy production, and communication, but these benefits can be realized only if nanotechnology is safe. In January 2012, the National Research Council reported that little progress has been made in understanding the health effects of nanotechnology and little research has been done on new nanotechnology products coming on the market. The federal government needs to create a master plan for risk research and to increase spending at least tenfold to ensure sufficient funding to carry out the plan.

When you finish your conclusion, read your introduction again. The main claim in your conclusion should be clearly related to the main subject, question, or claim in your introduction. If they do not match, revise your introduction so that it prepares your readers for where you will end. Your thinking evolves and develops as you write; thus often you need to adjust your introduction if you wrote it first.

4

Constructing an Argument

Imagine that you bought a new car in June and you are taking some of your friends to your favorite lake over the Fourth of July weekend. You have a great time until, as you are heading home, a drunk driver—a repeat offender—swerves into your lane and totals your new car. You and your friends are lucky not to be hurt, but you're outraged because you believe that repeat offenders should be prevented from driving, even if that means putting them in jail. You also remember going to another state that had sobriety checkpoints on holiday weekends. If such a checkpoint had been at the lake, you might still be driving your new car. You live in a town that encourages citizens to contribute to the local newspaper, and you think you could get a guest editorial published. The question is, how do you want to write the editorial?

- You could tell your story about how a repeat drunk driver endangered the lives of you and your friends.

- You could define driving while intoxicated (DWI) as a more legally culpable crime.

- You could compare the treatment of drunk drivers in your state with the treatment of drunk drivers in another state.

- You could cite statistics that alcohol-related accidents killed nearly 11,000 people in the United States in 2009.

- You could evaluate the present drunk-driving laws as insufficiently just or less than totally successful.

- You could propose taking vehicles away from repeat drunk drivers and forcing them to serve mandatory sentences.

- You could argue that your community should have sobriety checkpoints at times when drunk drivers are likely to be on the road.

- You could do several of the given points.

You're not going to have much space in the newspaper, so you decide to argue for sobriety checkpoints. You know that they are controversial. One of your friends who was in the car with you said that the checkpoints are unconstitutional because they involve search without probable cause. However, after doing some research to find out whether checkpoints are defined as legal or illegal, you learn that on June 14, 1990, the U.S. Supreme Court upheld the constitutionality of using checkpoints as a deterrent and enforcement tool against drunk drivers.

But you still want to know whether most people would agree with your friend that sobriety checkpoints are an invasion of privacy. You find opinion polls and surveys going back to the 1980s that show that 70 to 80 percent of those polled support sobriety checkpoints. You also realize that you can argue by analogy that security checkpoints for alcohol are similar in many ways to airport security checkpoints that protect passengers. You decide you will finish by making an argument from consequence. If people who go to the lake with plans to drink know in advance that there will be checkpoints, they will find a designated driver or some other means of safe transportation, and everyone else will also be safer.

The point of this example is that people very rarely set out to define something in an argument for the sake of definition, to compare for the sake of comparison, or to adopt any of the other ways of structuring an argument. Instead, they have a purpose in mind, and they use the kinds of arguments that are discussed in this chapter—most often in combination—as means to an end. Most arguments use multiple approaches and multiple sources of good reasons. Proposal arguments in particular often analyze a present situation with definition, causal, and evaluative arguments before advancing a course of future action to address that situation. The advantage of thinking explicitly about the structure of arguments is that you often find other ways to argue. Sometimes you just need a way to get started writing about complex issues.

DEFINITION ARGUMENTS

The continuing controversies about what should be defined as art, free speech, pornography, and hate crimes (to name just a few) illustrate why definitions often matter more than we might think. People argue about definitions because of the consequences of something being defined in a certain way. The controversies about certain subjects also illustrate three important principles that operate when definitions are used in arguments.

First, people make definitions that benefit their interests. Early in life you learned the importance of defining actions as "accidents." Windows can be broken through carelessness, especially when you are tossing a ball against the side of the house, but if it's an "accident," well, accidents just happen (and don't require punishment).

Second, most of the time when you are arguing about a definition, your audience will either have a different definition in mind or be unsure of the definition. Your mother or father probably didn't think breaking the window was an accident but rather was carelessness, so you had to convince Mom or Dad that you were really being careful, and the ball just slipped out of your hand. It's your job to get them to accept your definition.

Third, if you can get your audience to accept your definition, then usually you succeed. For this reason, definition arguments as a rule are the most powerful arguments.

Understand How Definition Arguments Work

Definition arguments set out criteria and then argue that whatever is being defined meets or does not meet those criteria.

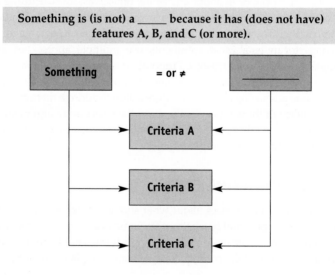

Something is (is not) a _____ because it has (does not have) features A, B, and C (or more).

Example

Graffiti is art because *it is a means of self expression, it shows an understanding of design principles,* and *it stimulates both the senses and the mind.*

Recognize Kinds of Definitions

Rarely do you get far into an argument without having to define something. Imagine that you are writing an argument about the decades-old and largely ineffective "war on drugs" in the United States. We all know that the war on drugs is being waged against drugs that are illegal, like cocaine and marijuana, and not against the legal drugs produced by the multibillion-dollar drug industry. Our society classifies drugs into two categories: "good" drugs, which are legal (though often controlled), and "bad" drugs, which are illegal.

How exactly does our society arrive at these definitions? Drugs would be relatively easy to define as good or bad if the difference could be defined at the molecular level. Bad drugs would contain certain molecules that define them as bad. The history of drug use in the United States, however, tells us that it is not so simple. In the twentieth century, alcohol was on the list of illegal drugs for over a decade, while opium was considered a good drug and was distributed in many patent medicines by pharmaceutical companies. Similarly, LSD (lysergic acid diethylamide) and MDMA (methylenedioxymethamphetamine, known better by its street name *ecstasy*) were developed by the pharmaceutical industry but later made illegal. In a few states, marijuana is now legal for medicinal use.

If drugs cannot be classified as good or bad by their molecular structure, then perhaps society classifies them by their effects. It might be reasonable to assume that addictive drugs are illegal, but that's not the case. Nicotine is highly addictive and is a legal drug, as are many prescription medicines. Drugs taken for the purpose of pleasure are not necessarily illegal (think of alcohol and Viagra), nor are drugs that alter consciousness or change personality (such as Prozac).

Whether a drug is defined as legal or illegal apparently is determined by example. The nationwide effort to stop Americans from drinking alcohol during the first decades of the twentieth century led to the passage of the Eighteenth Amendment and the ban on sales of alcohol from 1920 to 1933, known as Prohibition. Those who argued for Prohibition used examples of drunkenness, especially among the poor, to show how alcohol broke up families and left mothers and children penniless in the street. Those who opposed Prohibition initially pointed to the consumption of beer and wine in many cultural traditions. Later they raised examples of the bad effects of Prohibition—the rise of organized crime, the increase in alcohol abuse, and the general disregard for laws.

When you make a definition argument, it's important to think about what kind of definition you will use.

- **Formal definitions** typically categorize an item into the next-higher classification and provide criteria that distinguish the item from other items within that classification. Most dictionary definitions are formal definitions. For example, fish are cold-blooded aquatic vertebrates that have jaws, fins, and scales and are distinguished from other cold-blooded aquatic vertebrates (such as sea snakes) by the presence of gills. If you can construct a formal definition with specific criteria that your audience will accept, then you will likely have a strong argument. The key is to get your audience to agree to your criteria.

- **Operational definitions** are often used when a concept cannot be easily defined by formal definitions. For example, researchers who study binge drinking among college students define a binge as five or more drinks in one sitting for a man, and four or more drinks for a woman. Some people think this standard is too low and should be raised to six to eight drinks to distinguish true problem drinkers from the general college population. No matter what the number, researchers must argue that the particular definition is one that suits the concept.

- **Definitions from example** are used for many human qualities such as honesty, courage, creativity, deceit, and love. Few would not call the firefighters who entered the World Trade Center on September 11, 2001, courageous. Most people would describe someone with a diagnosis of terminal cancer who refuses to feel self-pity as courageous. But what about a student who declines to go to a concert with her friends so she can study for an exam? Her behavior might be admirable, but most people would hesitate to call it courageous. The key to arguing a definition from example is that the examples must strike the audience as typical of the concept, even if the situation is unusual.

Build a Definition Argument

Because definition arguments are so powerful, they are found at the center of some of the most important debates in American history. Definition arguments were at the heart of the abolition of slavery, for example, and many of the major arguments of the civil rights movement were based on definitions. Martin Luther King Jr.'s "Letter from Birmingham Jail" is one eloquent example.

King was jailed in April 1963 for leading a series of peaceful protests in Birmingham, Alabama. While he was being held in solitary confinement, Rev. King wrote a letter to eight white Birmingham clergymen. These religious leaders had issued a statement urging an end to the protests in their city. King argued that it was necessary to act now rather than wait for change. His purpose in writing the argument was to win acceptance for the protests and protestors and to make his audience see that the anti-segregationists were not agitators and rabble-rousers, but citizens acting responsibly to correct a grave injustice. A critical part of King's argument is his definition of "just" and "unjust" laws.

Supporters of segregation in Birmingham had obtained a court order forbidding further protests, and the eight white clergymen urged King and his supporters to obey the courts. Our society generally assumes that laws, and the courts that enforce them, should be obeyed. King, however, argues that there are two categories of laws and that citizens must treat one category differently from the other. Morally just laws, King argues, should be obeyed, but unjust ones should not. But how are just laws to be distinguished from unjust ones? By distinguishing two different kinds of laws, King creates a rationale for obeying some laws and disobeying others.

His argument rests on the clear moral and legal criteria he uses to define just and unjust laws. Without these criteria, people could simply disobey any law they chose, which is what King's detractors accused him of advocating. King had to show that he was in fact acting on principle, and that he and his supporters wanted to establish justice, not cause chaos. First, King states that a "just law is a man-made code that squares with the moral law of God" and "an unjust law is a code that is out of harmony with the moral law." Second, King notes that "any law that degrades human personality is unjust." Finally, King states that just laws are ones that hold for everyone because they were arrived at through democratic processes, while unjust laws are those that are inflicted on a minority that, because they were not permitted to vote, had no participation in approving them.

The definitions that King offers promote his goals. He maintains in his famous "Letter" that people have a moral responsibility to obey just laws, and, by the same logic, "a moral responsibility to disobey unjust laws." He then completes his definitional argument by showing how segregation laws fit the definition of "unjust" that he has laid out. Once his audience accepts his placement of segregation laws in the "unjust" category, they must also accept that King and his fellow protestors were right to break those laws. He answers to his critics effectively through a powerful definition argument.

Note how King's three definitions all fit the structure described at the beginning of this chapter:

> **Something is (or is not) a _____ because it has (does not have)**
> **features A,B, and C.**

Building an extended definition argument like King's is a two-step process. First, you have to establish the criteria for the categories you wish to define. In King's letter, consistency with moral law and uplifting of the human spirit are set forth as criteria for a just law. King provides arguments from St. Thomas Aquinas, a religious authority likely to carry significant weight with Birmingham clergymen and others who will read the letter.

Second, you must convince your audience that the particular case in question meets or doesn't meet the criteria. King cannot simply state that segregation laws are unjust; he must provide evidence showing how they fail to meet the criteria for a just law. Specifically, he notes the segregation "gives the segregator a false sense of superiority and the segregated a false sense of inferiority." These false senses of self are a distortion or degradation of the human personality.

Sometimes definition arguments have to argue for the relevance and suitability of the criteria. King, in fact, spent a great deal of his letter laying out and defending his criteria for just and unjust laws. While he addressed his letter to clergymen, he knew that it would find a wider audience. Therefore, he did not rely solely on criteria linked to moral law, or to Thomas Aquinas, or the "law of God." People who were not especially religious might not be convinced by those parts of his argument. So, King presents two additional criteria for just laws that he knows will appeal to those who value the democratic process.

When you build a definition argument, often you must put much effort into identifying and explaining your criteria. You must convince your readers that your criteria are the best ones for what you are defining and that they apply to the case you are arguing.

KING'S EXTENDED DEFINITION ARGUMENT

After establishing criteria for two kinds of laws, *just* and *unjust*, King argues that citizens must respond differently to laws that are unjust, by disobeying them. He then shows how the special case of *segregation laws* meets the criteria for unjust laws. If readers accept his argument, they will agree that segregation laws belong in the category of unjust laws, and therefore must be disobeyed.

Criteria for Just Laws	Criteria for Unjust Laws	Segregation Laws
Consistent with moral law	Not consistent with moral law	✓
Uplift human personality	Damage human personality	✓
Must be obeyed by all people	Must be obeyed by some people, but not others	✓
Made by democratically elected representatives	Not made by democratically elected representatives	✓
Appropriate response to just laws: All citizens should obey them.	Appropriate response to unjust laws: All citizens should disobey them.	

SAMPLE STUDENT DEFINITION ARGUMENT

Conley 1

Patrice Conley
Professor Douglas
English 101
28 April 2012

Flagrant Foul: The NCAA's Definition of Student
Athletes as Amateurs

Every year, thousands of student athletes across
America sign the National Collegiate Athletic Association's
Form 08-3a, the "Student-Athlete" form, waiving their
right to receive payment for the use of their name and
image (McCann). The form defines student athletes as
amateurs, who cannot receive payment for playing their
sports. While their schools and coaches may make millions
of dollars in salaries and endorsement deals and are the
highest-paid public employees in many states, student
athletes can never earn a single penny from their college
athletic careers. Former Nike executive Sonny Vacarro
sums it up: "Everybody has a right except for the player.
The player has no rights" ("Money").

Make no mistake: college athletics are big business.
The most visible college sports—big-time men's football
and basketball—generate staggering sums of money.
For example, the twelve universities in the Southeastern
Conference receive $205 million each year from CBS
and ESPN for the right to broadcast its football games
(Smith and Ourand). Even more money comes in from
video games, clothing, and similar licenses. In 2010, the
New York Times reported, "the NCAA's licensing deals
are estimated at more than $4 billion" per year (Thamel).

Conley 2

While the staggering executive pay at big corporations has brought public outrage, coaches' salaries are even more outlandish. Kentucky basketball coach, John Calipari, is paid over $4 million a year for a basketball program that makes about $35-40 million a year, more than 10% of the entire revenue. Tom Van Riper observes that no corporate CEO commands this large a share of the profits. He observes that if Steve Ballmer, the CEO at Microsoft, had Calipari's deal, Ballmer would make over $6 billion a year.

How can colleges allow advertisers, arena operators, concession owners, athletic gear manufacturers, retailers, game companies, and media moguls, along with coaches and university officials, to make millions and pay the stars of the show nothing? The answer is that colleges define athletes as amateurs. Not only are student athletes not paid for playing their sport, they cannot receive gifts and are not allowed to endorse products, which may be a violation of their right to free speech. The NCAA, an organization of colleges and schools, forces student athletes to sign away their rights because, it says, it is protecting the students. If student athletes could accept money from anyone, the NCAA argues, they might be exploited, cheated, or even bribed. Taking money out of the equation is supposed to let students focus on academics and preserve the amateur status of college sports.

The definition of amateur arose in the nineteenth century in Britain, when team sports became popular. Middle-class and upper-class students in college had ample time to play their sports while working-class athletes had only a half-day off (no sports were played on Sundays in that era). Teams began to pay top working-class sportsmen for the time they had to take off from work. Middle-class and upper-class sportsmen didn't want to play against the working-class teams, so they made the distinction between amateurs and professionals. The definition of amateur crossed the Atlantic to the United States, where college sports became popular in the 1880s. But it was not long until the hypocrisy of amateurism undermined the ideal. Top football programs like Yale had slush funds to pay athletes, and others used ringers—players who weren't students—and even players from other schools (Zimbalist 7).

The Olympic Games maintained the amateur-professional distinction until 1988, but it was long evident that Communist bloc nations were paying athletes to train full-time and Western nations were paying athletes through endorsement contracts. The only Olympic sport that now requires amateur status is boxing. The college sports empire in the United States run by the NCAA is the last bastion of amateurism for sports that draw audiences large enough to be televised.

Colleges might be able to defend the policy of amateurism if they extended this definition to all students. A fair policy is one that treats all students the same. A fair policy doesn't result in some students getting paid for professional work, while other students do not. Consider the students in the Butler School of Music at the University of Texas at Austin, for example. Many student musicians perform at the professional level. Does the school prevent them from earning money for their musical performances? No. In fact, the school runs a referral service that connects its students with people and businesses who want to hire

Conley 4

professional musicians. The university even advises its
students on how to negotiate a contract and get paid for
their performance ("Welcome").

Likewise, why are student actors and actresses allowed
to earn money from their work and images, while student
athletes are not? Think about actress Emma Watson, who
enrolled at Brown University in Rhode Island. Can you
imagine the university officials at Brown telling Watson
that she would have to make the next two Harry Potter
films for free, instead of for the $5 million she has been
offered? Can you imagine Brown University telling Watson
that all the revenue from Harry Potter merchandise bearing
her likeness would have to be paid directly to the university, for the rest of her life? They would if Watson were an
athlete instead of an actress.

In fact, compared to musicians and actors, student
athletes have an even greater need to earn money while
they are still in college. Athletes' professional careers
are likely to be much shorter than musicians' or actors'.
College may be the only time some athletes have the opportunity to capitalize on their success. (Indeed, rather than
focusing student athletes on their academic careers, the
NCAA policy sometimes forces students to leave college
early, so they can earn a living before their peak playing
years are over.) Student athletes often leave school with
permanent injuries and no medical insurance or job pros-
pects, whereas student musicians and actors rarely suffer
career-ending injuries on the job.

Student athletes are prevented from profiting from
their name and image. The NCAA says this rule preserves
their standing as amateurs and protects them from the

celebrity and media frenzy surrounding professional sports stars. Search for a "Tim Tebow Jersey" online, and you can buy officially branded Florida Gators shirts, ranging in price from $34.99 to $349.99 (autographed by Tebow). The NCAA, the University of Florida, Nike, and the other parties involved in the production and sale of these products get around the problem of using an amateur's name by using his team number instead. Tebow's name doesn't appear anywhere on the jerseys—just his number, fifteen. Yet all these jerseys are identified as "Official Tim Tebow Gators merchandise," and they are certainly bought by fans of Tebow rather than people who just happen to like the number fifteen. Nobody is saying how much money these jerseys have made for Nike, or for the University of Florida. What we do know for sure is the amount Tim Tebow has made off the jerseys: nothing.

Defenders of the current system argue that student athletes on scholarships are paid with free tuition, free room and board, free books, and tutoring help. The total package can be the equivalent of $120,000 over four years. For those student athletes who are motivated to take advantage of the opportunity, the lifetime benefits can be enormous. Unfortunately, too few student athletes do take advantage of the opportunity. Seldom does a major college football and men's basketball program have a graduation rate at or close to the overall student body. A study by the University of North Carolina's College Sports Research Institute released in 2010 accuses the NCAA of playing fast and loose with graduation rates by counting part-time students in statistics for the general student body, which makes graduation rates for athletes look better in a

Conley 6

comparison. Student athletes must be full-time students; thus they should be compared to other full-time students. The North Carolina Institute reports that 54.8% of major college (Football Bowl Subdivision) football players at 117 schools graduated within six years, compared to 73.7% of other full-time students. The gap between basketball players was even greater, with 44.6% of athletes graduating compared to 75.7% of the general student body (Zaiger). For the handful of talented athletes who can play in the National Football League or the National Basketball Association, college sports provide training for their future lucrative, although short-lived, profession. But as the NCAA itself points out in its ads, the great majority of student athletes "go pro in something other than sports." For the 55% of college basketball players who fail to graduate, the supposed $120,000 package is an air ball.

The NCAA would be wise to return to the older definition of amateur, which comes from Latin through old French, meaning "lover of." It doesn't necessarily have to have anything to do with money. Whether it's a jazz performer or dancer or an athlete, an amateur ought to be considered someone in love with an activity—someone who cares deeply about the activity, studies the activity in depth, and practices in order to be highly proficient. NBA players, Olympians, college athletes, high school players, and even bird watchers, star gazers, and open-source programmers: they're all amateurs. If they are lucky enough to be paid, so be it.

Conley 7

Works Cited

McCann, Michael. "NCAA Faces Unspecified Damages, Changes in Latest Anti-Trust Case." *SI.com.* Time, Inc., 21 July 2009. Web. 6 Apr. 2012.

"Money and March Madness." *Frontline.* PBS, 29 Mar. 2011. Web. 3 Apr. 2012.

National Collegiate Athletic Association. Advertisement. *NCAA.org.* NCAA, 13 Mar. 2007. Web. 3 Apr. 2012.

Smith, Michael, and John Ourand. "ESPN Pays $2.25B for SEC Rights." *SportsBusiness Journal.* Smith and Street, 25 Aug. 2008. Web. 1 Apr. 2012.

Thamel, Pete. "N.C.A.A. Fails to Stop Licensing Lawsuit." *New York Times.* New York Times, 8 Feb. 2010. Web. 1 Apr. 2012.

Van Riper, Thomas. "The Highest-Paid College Basketball Coaches." *Forbes.com.* Forbes, 8 Mar. 2010. Web. 6 Apr. 2012.

"Welcome to the Music Referral Service." *Butler School of Music.* Univ. of Texas at Austin, n.d. Web. 5 Apr. 2012.

Zaiger, Alan Scher. "Study: NCAA Graduation Rate Comparisons Flawed." *ABC News.* ABC News, 20 Apr. 2010. Web. 1 Apr. 2012.

Zimbalist, Andrew. *Unpaid Professionals: Commercialism and Conflict in Big-Time College Sports.* Princeton UP, 2001. Print.

WRITE A DEFINITION ARGUMENT

Step 1 Make a claim

Make a definitional claim on a controversial issue that focuses on a key term.

Template

_____ is (or is not) a _____ because it has (or does not have) features A, B, and C (or more).

Examples

- Hate speech (or pornography, literature, films, and so on) is (or is not) free speech protected by the First Amendment because it has (or does not have) these features.

- Hunting (or using animals for cosmetics testing, keeping animals in zoos, wearing furs, and so on) is (or is not) cruelty to animals because it has (or does not have) these features.

Step 2 Think about what's at stake

- Does nearly everyone agree with you? If so, then your claim probably isn't interesting or important. If you can think of people who disagree, then something is at stake.

- Who argues the opposite of your claim?

- Why or how do they benefit from a different definition?

Step 3 List the criteria

- Which criteria are necessary for _____ to be a _____?

- Which are not necessary?

- Which are the most important?

- Does your case in point meet all the criteria?

Step 4 Analyze your potential readers

- Who are your readers?

- How does the definitional claim you are making affect them?

- How familiar are they with the issue, concept, or controversy that you're writing about?

- What are they likely to know and not know?
- Which criteria are they most likely to accept with little explanation, and which will they disagree with?

Step 5 Write a draft

Introduction
- Set out the issue, concept, or controversy.
- Give the background that your intended readers need.

Body
- Set out your criteria and argue for the appropriateness of the criteria.
- Determine whether the criteria apply to the case in point.
- Anticipate where readers might question either your criteria or how they apply to your subject.
- Address opposing viewpoints by acknowledging how their definitions differ and by showing why your definition is better.

Conclusion
- Do more than simply summarize. You can, for example, go into more detail about what is at stake or the implications of your definition.

Step 6 Revise, edit, proofread

- For detailed instructions, see Chapter 7.
- For a checklist to use to evaluate your draft, see pages 180–182.

CAUSAL ARGUMENTS

Why did the driver who passed you on a blind curve risk his life to get one car ahead at the next traffic light? Why is it hard to recognize people you know when you run into them unexpectedly in an unfamiliar setting? Why does your mother or father spend an extra hour, plus the extra gas, driving to a supermarket across town just to save a few pennies on one or two items on sale? Why do some of your friends keep going to horror films when they can hardly sit through them and have nightmares afterward?

Life is full of big and little mysteries, and people spend a lot of time speculating about the causes. Most of the time, however, they don't take the time to analyze in depth what causes a controversial trend, event, or phenomenon. But in college and in the workplace, you likely will have to write causal arguments that require in-depth analysis. In a professional career you will have to make many detailed causal analyses: Why did a retail business fail when it seemed to have an ideal location? What causes cost overruns in the development of a new product? What causes people in some circumstances to prefer public transportation over driving?

Understand How Causal Arguments Work

Causal arguments take three basic forms.

1. One cause leads to one or more effects.

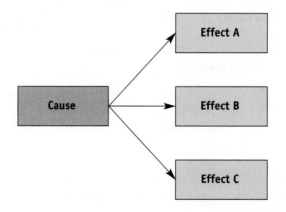

Example

The **invention of the telegraph** led to the *commodities market, the establishment of standard time zones*, and *news reporting as we know it today.*

2. One effect has several causes.

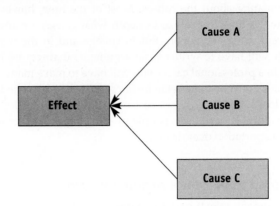

Example

Hurricanes are becoming more financially destructive to the United States because of *the greater intensity of recent storms, an increase in the commercial and residential development of coastal areas,* and *a reluctance to enforce certain construction standards in coastal residential areas.*

3. Something causes something else to happen, which in turn causes something else to happen.

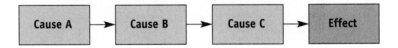

Example

Making the HPV vaccination mandatory for adolescent girls will make *unprotected sex seem safer, leading to greater promiscuity,* and **resulting in more teenage pregnancies**.

Find Causes

The causal claim is at the center of a causal argument. Therefore, to get started on a causal argument, you need to propose one or more causes. The big problem with causal arguments is that any topic worth writing about is likely to be complex, making identifying causes difficult. The philosopher John Stuart Mill recognized this problem long ago and devised four methods for finding causes:

- **The Common Factor Method.** Sometimes causes can be identified because two or more similar events share a common factor. The common factor may be the cause. For example, if two people in two different states both develop a rare disease, and both of them recently traveled to Madagascar, they were probably exposed to the illness while there.

- **The Single Difference Method.** Causes can often be identified when two situations or events have different outcomes. If there is a single difference in the two scenarios, that difference may be the cause. At the 1998 Winter Olympics in Nagano, Japan, the speed skating team from the Netherlands introduced a technological innovation to the sport—clap skates, which improve skaters' performance by keeping the skate blade in contact with the ice longer. Racing against the best skaters in the world, the Dutch on their clap skates won eleven of thirty medals, five of which were gold. By the 2002 Winter Olympics, all speed skaters had switched over to the new skates, and the medal count was much more evenly distributed. That year the United States, the Netherlands, and Germany each won three gold medals, and a total of eight medals apiece. Clap skates were the most likely cause of the Netherlands' dominance four years earlier.

- **Concomitant Variation.** Some causes are discovered by observing a shared pattern of variation in a possible cause and possible effect. For example, scientists noticed that peaks in the eleven-year sunspot cycle have predictable effects on high-frequency radio transmission on the earth.

- **Process of Elimination.** Many possible causes can be proposed for most trends and events. If you are a careful investigator, you have to consider all causes that you can think of and eliminate the ones that cannot be causes.

To understand how these methods might work for you, consider this example. Suppose you want to research the causes of the increase in legalized lotteries in the United States. You might discover that lotteries go back to colonial times. Lotteries were common before and after the American Revolution, but they eventually ran into trouble because they were run by private companies that failed to pay the winners. After 1840, laws against lotteries were passed, but they came back in the South after the Civil War. The defeated states of the Confederacy needed money to rebuild the bridges, buildings, and schools that were destroyed in the Civil War, and they turned to selling lottery tickets throughout the nation (ironically, the tickets were very popular in the North). Once again, the lotteries were run by private companies, and scandals eventually led to their being banned.

In 1964, the voters in New Hampshire approved a lottery as a means of funding education—in preference to an income tax or a sales tax. Soon other northeastern states followed this lead and established lotteries with the reasoning that if people were going to gamble, the money should remain at home. During the 1980s, other states approved not only lotteries but also other forms of state-run gambling such as keno and video poker. By 1993, only Hawaii and Utah had no legalized gambling of any kind.

If you are analyzing the causes of the spread of legalized gambling, you might use the **common factor method** to investigate what current lotteries have in common with earlier lotteries. That factor is easy to identify: it's economic. The early colonies and later the states have turned to lotteries again and again as a way of raising money that avoids unpopular tax increases. But why have lotteries spread so quickly and seemingly become so permanent since 1964, when before that, they were used only sporadically and were banned eventually? The **single difference method** points us to the major difference between the lotteries of today and those of previous eras: Lotteries in the past were run by private companies, and inevitably someone took off with the money instead of paying it out. Today's lotteries are owned and operated by state agencies or contracted under state control, and while they are not immune to scandals, they are much more closely monitored than lotteries were in the past.

Many effects don't have causes as obvious as the spread of legalized gambling. The **process of elimination method** can be a useful tool when several possible causes are involved. Perhaps you have had the experience of your television not turning on. To identify the problem, if you checked first to see if it was plugged in, then plugged it into another socket to make sure the socket was on, and then checked the surge suppressor to see if it worked, you used a process of elimination to diagnose the cause of the problem. Major advances in science and medicine have resulted from the process of elimination. For centuries, soldiers on long campaigns and sailors on long sea voyages suffered horrible deaths from scurvy until 1747, when James Lind demonstrated that scurvy could be treated and prevented with a diet that includes lemons and limes. Nevertheless, people proposed various causes for scurvy including poor hygiene, lack of exercise, and tainted canned food. Finally, in 1932, the cause of scurvy was proven to be a vitamin C deficiency.

Build a Causal Argument

A pitfall common in causal arguments using statistics is mistaking correlation for causation. For example, the FBI reported that in 1995 criminal victimization rates in the United States dropped 13 percent for personal crimes and 12.4 percent for property crimes—the largest decreases ever. During that same year, the nation's prison and jail populations reached a record high of 1,085,000 and 507,000 inmates, respectively. The easy inference is that putting more people behind bars lowers the crime rate, but there are plenty of examples to the contrary. The drop in crime rates in the 1990s remains quite difficult to explain.

Others have argued that the decline in SAT verbal scores during the late 1960s and 1970s reflected a decline in literacy skills caused by an increase in television viewing. But the fact that the number of people who took the SAT during the 1970s greatly increased suggests that the major cause was a great expansion in the population who wanted to go to college.

SAMPLE STUDENT CAUSAL ARGUMENT

Armadi Tansal
Professor Stewart
English 115
28 October 2011

Modern Warfare: Video Games' Link to
Real-World Violence

"John" is a nineteen-year-old college student who gets decent grades. He comes from a typical upper-middle-class family and plans to get his MBA after he graduates. John is also my friend, which is why I'm not using his real name.

John has been playing moderately violent video games since he was nine years old. I started playing video and console games around that age too, and I played a lot in junior high, but John plays more than anyone I know. John says that over the past year he has played video games at least four hours every day, and "sometimes all day and night on the weekends." I have personally witnessed John play *Call of Duty: Modern Warfare 2* for six hours straight, with breaks only to use the bathroom or eat something.

I've never seen John act violently, and he's never been in trouble with the law. But new research on violent video games suggests that John's gaming habit puts him at risk for violent or aggressive behavior. Dr. Craig Anderson, a psychologist at the University of Iowa, says "the active role required by video games...may make violent video games even more hazardous than violent television or cinema" (Anderson). When people like John play these games, they get used to being rewarded for violent behavior. For example, in the multiplayer version of *Modern Warfare 2,* if the player gets a five-kill streak, he can call in a Predator missile strike. If you kill twenty-five people in a row, you can call in a tactical nuclear strike. Missile strikes help you advance toward the mission goals more quickly, so the more people you kill, the faster you'll win.

Along with *Modern Warfare 2,* John plays games like *Left 4 Dead, Halo,* and *Grand Theft Auto.* All these games are rated M for Mature, which according to the Entertainment Software Rating Board means they "may contain intense violence, blood and gore, sexual content and/ or strong language." Some M-rated games, like *Grand Theft Auto,* feature random violence, where players can run amok in a city, beat up and kill people, and smash stuff for no reason. In others, like *Modern Warfare 2,* the violence takes place in the context of military action. To do well in all of these games, you have to commit acts of violence. But does acting violently in games make you more violent in real life?

Anderson says studies show that "violent video games are significantly associated with: increased aggressive behavior, thoughts, and affect [feelings]; increased physio-logical arousal; and decreased prosocial (helping) behavior" (Anderson). He also claims that "high levels of violent video game exposure have been linked to delinquency, fighting at school and during free play periods, and violent criminal behavior (e.g., self-reported assault, robbery)."

Being "associated with" and "linked to" violent behavior doesn't necessarily mean video games cause such behavior. Many people have argued that the links Anderson sees are coincidental, or that any effects video games might have on behavior are so slight that we shouldn't worry about

Tansal 3

them. Christopher Ferguson and John Kilburn, professors of criminal justice at Texas A&M International University, feel that the existing research does not support Anderson's claims. In a report published in the *Journal of Pediatrics,* they point out that in past studies, "the closer aggression measures got to actual violent behavior, the weaker the effects seen."

From what I can tell, John doesn't have any more violent thoughts and feelings than most men his age. When I asked him if he thought the games had made him more violent or aggressive in real life, he said, "I'm actually less violent now. When we were kids we used to play 'war' with fake guns and sticks, chasing each other around the neighborhood and fighting commando-style. We didn't really fight but sometimes kids got banged up. No one ever gets hurt playing a video game."

Anderson admits that "a healthy, normal, nonviolent child or adolescent who has no other risk factors for high aggression or violence is not going to become a school shooter simply because they play five hours or 10 hours a week of these violent video games" (qtd. in St. George). But just because violent video games don't turn all players into mass murderers, that doesn't mean they have no effect on a player's behavior and personality. For example, my friend John doesn't get into fights or rob people, but he doesn't display a lot of prosocial "helping" behaviors either. He spends most of his free time gaming, so he doesn't get out of his apartment much. Also, the friends he does have mostly play video games with him.

Even though the games restrict his interactions with other humans and condition him to behave violently onscreen, John is probably not at high risk of becoming violent in real life. But according to researchers, this low risk of becoming violent is because none of the dozens of other risk factors associated with violent behavior are present in his life (Anderson et al. 160). If John were a high school dropout, came from a broken home, or abused alcohol and other drugs, his game playing might be more likely to contribute to violent behavior.

Anderson contends that violent video games are a "causal risk factor" for violence and aggression—not that they alone cause violent aggression. In other words, the games are a small piece of a much larger problem. People like my friend John are not likely to become violent because of the video games they play. But Anderson's research indicates that some people do. Although there is no simple way to tell who those people are, we should include video games as a possible risk factor when we think about who is likely to become violent.

Even if the risk contributed by violent video games is slight for each individual, the total impact of the games on violence in society could be huge. *Call of Duty: Modern Warfare 2* is the third-best-selling video game in the United States (Orry). Its creator, Activision Blizzard, had $1.3 billion in sales in the just first three months of 2010 (Pham). Millions of people play this game and games like it, and they aren't all as well-adjusted as John. If video games contribute to violent tendencies in only a small fraction of players, they could still have a terrible impact.

Tansal 5

Works Cited

Anderson, Craig. "Violent Video Games: Myths, Facts, and Unanswered Questions." *Psychological Science Agenda* 16.5 (2003): n. pag. Web. 6 Oct. 2011.

Anderson, Craig, et al. "Violent Video Game Effects on Aggression, Empathy, and Prosocial Behavior in Eastern and Western Countries." *Psychological Bulletin* 136.2 (2010): 151–73. Print.

Entertainment Software Rating Board. *Game Ratings and Descriptor Guide.* Entertainment Software Association, n.d. Web. 7 Oct. 2011.

Ferguson, Christopher J., and John Kilburn. "The Public Health Risks of Media Violence: A Meta-Analytic Review." *Journal of Pediatrics* 154.5 (2009): 759–63. Print.

John (pseudonym). Personal interview. 4 Oct. 2011.

Orry, James. "Modern Warfare 2 the 3rd Best-Selling Game in the US." *Videogamer.com.* Pro-G Media Ltd., 12 Mar. 2010. Web. 6 Oct. 2011.

Pham, Alex. "Call of Duty: Modern Warfare 2 Propels Revenue, Profit for Activision Blizzard." *Los Angeles Times.* Los Angeles Times, 6 May 2010. Web. 7 Oct. 2011.

St. George, Donna. "Study Links Violent Video Games, Hostility." *Washington Post.* Washington Post, 3 Nov. 2008. Web. 5 Oct. 2011.

WRITE A CAUSAL ARGUMENT

Step 1 Make a claim

Make a causal claim on a controversial trend, event, or phenomenon.

Template

SOMETHING does (or does not) cause SOMETHING ELSE.
-or-
SOMETHING causes SOMETHING ELSE, which, in turn, causes SOMETHING ELSE.

Examples

- One-parent families (or television violence, bad diet, and so on) are (or are not) the cause of emotional and behavioral problems in children.

- Firearms control laws (or right-to-carry-handgun laws) reduce (or increase) violent crimes.

- Putting grade school children into competitive sports teaches them how to succeed in later life (or puts undue emphasis on winning and teaches many who are slower to mature to have a negative self-image).

Step 2 What's at stake in your claim

- If the cause is obvious to everyone, then it probably isn't worth writing about.

Step 3 Think of possible causes

- Which are the immediate causes?
- Which are the background causes?
- Which are the hidden causes?

Step 4 Analyze your potential readers

- Who are your readers?
- How familiar are they with the trend, event, or phenomenon that you're writing about?
- What are they likely to know and not know?
- How likely are they to accept your causal explanation?
- What alternative explanation might they argue for?

Step 5 Write a draft

Introduction
- Describe the controversial trend, event, or phenomenon.
- Give the background that your intended readers need.

Body
- Explain the circumstances of a trend, event, or phenomenon that are unfamiliar to your readers. Remember that providing facts is not the same thing as establishing causes, although facts can help to support your causal analysis.
- Set out the causes that have been offered and reject them one by one. Then you can present the cause that you think is most important.
- Treat a series of causes one by one, analyzing the importance of each.

Conclusion
- Do more than simply summarize. Consider describing additional effects beyond those that have been noted previously.

Step 6 Revise, edit, proofread
- For detailed instructions, see Chapter 7.
- For a checklist to use to evaluate your draft, see pages 180–182.

EVALUATION ARGUMENTS

People make evaluations all the time. Newspapers and magazines have picked up on this love of evaluation by running "best of" polls. They ask their readers to vote on the best Chinese restaurant, the best pizza, the best local band, the best coffeehouse, the best dance club, the best neighborhood park, the best swimming hole, the best bike ride (scenic or challenging), the best volleyball court, the best place to get married, and so on. If you ask one of your friends who voted in a "best" poll why she picked a particular restaurant as the best of its kind, she might respond by saying simply, "I like it." But if you ask her why she likes it, she might start offering good reasons such as these: the food is good, the service prompt, the prices fair, and the atmosphere comfortable. It's really not a mystery why these polls are often quite predictable or why the same restaurants tend to win year after year. Many people think that evaluations are matters of personal taste, but when we begin probing the reasons, we often discover that different people use similar criteria to make evaluations.

The key to convincing other people that your judgment is sound is establishing the criteria you will use to make your evaluation. Sometimes it will be necessary to argue for the validity of the criteria that you think your readers should consider. If your readers accept your criteria, it's likely they will agree with your conclusions.

Understand How Evaluation Arguments Work

Evaluation arguments set out criteria and then judge something to be good or bad or best or worst according to those criteria.

> **Something is a good (bad, the best, the worst) _____ if measured by certain criteria (practicality, aesthetics, ethics).**

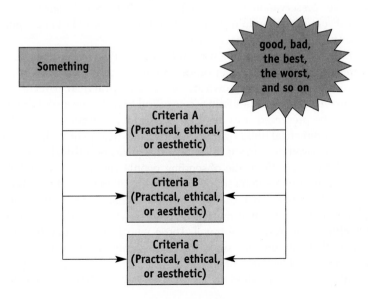

Example

Google Maps is the best mapping program because *it is easy to use, it is accurate,* and *it provides entertaining and educational features such as Google Earth.*

Recognize Kinds of Evaluations

Arguments of evaluation are structured much like arguments of definition. Recall that the criteria in arguments of definition are set out in *because* clauses: SOMETHING is a _____ because it has these criteria. The key move in writing most evaluative arguments is first deciding what kind of criteria to use.

Imagine that the oldest commercial building in your city is about to be torn down. Your goal is to get the old store converted to a museum by making a proposal argument. First you will need to make an evaluative argument that will form the basis of your proposal. You might argue that a downtown museum would be much better than more office space because it would draw more visitors. You might argue that the stonework in the building is of excellent quality and deserves preservation. Or you might argue that it is only fair that the oldest commercial building be preserved because the oldest house and other historic buildings have been saved.

Each of these arguments uses different criteria. An argument that a museum is better than an office building because it would bring more visitors to the downtown area is based on **practical criteria**. An argument that the old building is beautiful and that beautiful things should be preserved uses **aesthetic criteria**. An argument that the oldest commercial building deserves the same treatment as the oldest house is based on fairness, a concept that relies on **ethical criteria**. The debate over the value of sending people versus sending robots into space employs all these criteria but with different emphases. Both those who favor and those who oppose human space travel make practical arguments that much scientific knowledge and many other benefits result from space travel. Those who favor sending humans use aesthetic arguments: space travel is essential to the way we understand ourselves as humans and Americans. Those who oppose sending humans question the ethics of spending so much money for manned space vehicles when there are pressing needs at home, and they point out that robots can be used for a fraction of the cost.

Build an Evaluation Argument

Most people have a lot of practice making consumer evaluations, and when they have enough time to do their homework, they usually make an informed decision. Sometimes, criteria for evaluations are not so obvious, however, and evaluations are much more difficult to make. Sometimes one set of criteria favors one choice, while another set of criteria favors another. You might have encountered this problem when you chose a college. If you were able to leave home to go to school, you had a potential choice of over 1600 accredited colleges and universities. Until thirty years ago, there wasn't much information about choosing a college other than what colleges said about themselves. You could find out the price of tuition and what courses were offered, but it was hard to compare one college with another.

In 1983, the magazine *U.S. News & World Report* began ranking U.S. colleges and universities from a consumer's perspective. These rankings have remained highly controversial ever since. Many college officials have attacked the criteria that *U.S. News* uses to make its evaluations, calling for a national boycott of the *U.S. News* rankings (without much success). *U.S. News* replies in its defense that colleges and universities themselves do a lot of ranking. Schools rank students for admissions, using SAT or ACT scores, high school GPA, high school class rank, quality of high school, and other factors, and then grade the students and rank them against each other when they are enrolled in college. Furthermore, schools also evaluate faculty members and take great interest in the national ranking of their departments. They care very much about where they stand in relation to each other. Why, then, *U.S. News* argues, shouldn't people be able to evaluate colleges and universities, since colleges and universities are so much in the business of evaluating people?

Arguing for the right to evaluate colleges and universities is one thing; actually doing comprehensive and reliable evaluations is quite another. *U.S. News* uses a formula in which about 25 percent of a school's ranking is based on a survey of reputation in which the president, provost, and dean of admissions at each college rate the quality of schools in the same category, and the remaining 75 percent is based on statistical criteria of quality. These statistical criteria fall into six major categories: retention of students, faculty resources, student selectivity, financial resources, alumni giving, and graduation rate performance—the difference between the number of students who are expected to graduate and the number that actually do. These major categories are made up of factors that are weighted according to their importance. For example, the faculty resources category is determined by the size of classes (the proportion of classes with fewer than twenty students to classes with fifty or more students), the average faculty pay weighted by the cost of living in different regions of the country, the percentage of professors with the highest degree in their field, the overall student-faculty ratio, and the percentage of faculty who are full-time.

Those who have challenged the *U.S. News* rankings argue that the magazine should use different criteria or weight the criteria differently. *U.S. News* explains its ranking system on its Web site (colleges.usnews.rankingsandreviews.com/best-colleges). If you are curious about where your school ranks, take a look.

WRITE AN EVALUATION ARGUMENT

Step 1 Make a claim

Make an evaluative claim based on specific criteria.

Template

> SOMETHING is good (bad, the best, the worst) if measured by certain criteria (practicality, aesthetics, ethics).

Examples

- A book or movie review.
- A defense of a particular kind of music or art.
- An evaluation of a controversial aspect of sports (e.g., the current system of determining who is champion in Division I college football by a system of bowls and polls) or a sports event (e.g., this year's WNBA playoffs) or a team.

- An evaluation of the effectiveness of an educational program (such as your high school honors program or your college's core curriculum requirement) or some other aspect of your campus.

- An evaluation of the effectiveness of a social policy or law such as legislating 21 as the legal drinking age, current gun control laws, or environmental regulation.

Step 2 Think about what's at stake

- Does nearly everyone agree with you? If so, then your claim probably isn't interesting or important. If you can think of people who disagree, then something is at stake.

- Who argues the opposite of your claim?

- Why do they make a different evaluation?

Step 3 List the criteria

- Which criteria make something either good or bad?

- Which are the most important?

- Which criteria are fairly obvious, and which will you have to argue for?

Step 4 Analyze your potential readers

- Who are your readers?

- How familiar are they with what you are evaluating?

- What are they likely to know and not know?

- Which criteria are they most likely to accept with little explanation, and which will they disagree with?

Step 5 Write a draft

Introduction

- Introduce the person, group, institution, event, or object that you are going to evaluate. You might want to announce your stance at this point or wait until the concluding section.

- Give the background that your intended readers need.

Body

- Describe each criterion and then analyze how well what you are evaluating meets that criterion.

- If you are making an evaluation according to the effects someone or something produces, describe each effect in detail.

- Anticipate where readers might question either your criteria or how they apply to your subject.

- Address opposing viewpoints by acknowledging how their evaluations might differ and by showing why your evaluation is better.

Conclusion

- If you have not yet announced your stance, conclude that, on the basis of the criteria you set out or the effects you have analyzed, something is good (bad, the best, the worst).

- If you have made your stance clear from the beginning, end with a compelling example or analogy.

Step 6 Revise, edit, proofread

- For detailed instructions, see Chapter 7.
- For a checklist to use to evaluate your draft, see pages 180–182.

REBUTTAL ARGUMENTS

When you hear the word *rebuttal*, you might think of a debate team or the part of a trial when the attorney for the defense answers the plaintiff's accusations. Although rebuttal has those definitions, a rebuttal argument can be thought of in much larger terms. Indeed, much of what people know about the world today is the result of centuries of arguments of rebuttal.

Understand How Rebuttal Arguments Work

When you rebut the argument of someone else, you can do one of two things. You can refute the argument, or you can counterargue. In the first case, **refutation**, you emphasize the shortcomings of the argument that you wish to undermine without really making a positive case of your own. In the second case, **counterargument**, you emphasize not the shortcomings of the argument that you are rebutting but the strengths of the position you wish to support. Often there is considerable overlap between refutation and counterargument, and often both are present in a rebuttal.

Refutation: The opposing argument has serious shortcomings that undermine the claim.

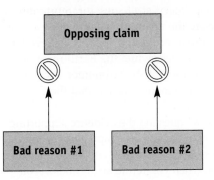

Example

The great white shark gained a reputation as a "man eater" from the 1975 movie *Jaws*, but in fact **attacks on humans are rare** and **most bites have been "test bites,"** which is a common shark behavior with unfamiliar objects.

Counterarguments: The opposing argument has some merit, but my argument is superior.

Example

Those who argue for tariffs on goods from China claim that tariffs will protect American manufacturing jobs, but **tariffs would increase prices on clothing, furniture, toys, and other consumer goods for everyone and would cause the loss of retailing jobs.**

Recognize Kinds of Rebuttal Arguments

Refutation

There are two primary strategies for refutation arguments. First, you can challenge the assumptions on which a claim is based. Until about five hundred years ago, people believed that the sky, and everything in it, moved, while the Earth remained still. In the early sixteenth century, the Polish astronomer Nicolaus Copernicus challenged this assumption and argued that the Earth and other planets circle around the Sun.

Second, you can question the evidence supporting the claim. Sometimes the evidence presented is simply wrong. Sometimes the evidence is incomplete or unrepresentative, and sometimes counterevidence can be found. Often when you refute an argument, you make the case that your opponent has been guilty of one or more fallacies of arguments (see pages 55–57). A lively debate has developed in recent years over the impacts of *Web 2.0*, a term that has come to stand for a Web-based social phenomenon characterized by open communication and a decentralization of authority. Various new genres and social media are associated with Web 2.0, including wikis, blogs, YouTube, Facebook, eBay, craigslist, Twitter—anything that encourages participation and can exist only on the Internet.

From the beginning the Internet inspired grand visions of a better society through access to information and instant communication. The initial enthusiasm declined after the Web turned into a giant home-shopping network and the potential for dialogue among different groups was lost in the proliferation of political and advocacy sites. But Web 2.0 rekindled that enthusiasm with the potential of connecting billions of human minds. Wikipedia is held up as a glorious example of the age of participation because it allows us to pool the collective wisdom of all our brains. Amateurism is celebrated. Anyone can publish writing, videos, songs, photographs, and other art for everyone else connected to the Internet to see and hear, and millions of people are doing just that.

Not surprisingly, the hype over Web 2.0 has drawn critics. In June 2007, Andrew Keen published *The Cult of the Amateur: How Today's*

Internet Is Killing Our Culture, which upholds the authority of the expert against the thousands of amateurs who contribute to YouTube and Wikipedia. He challenges the assumptions of those who inflate the promise of Web 2.0:

> The Web 2.0 revolution has peddled the promise of bringing more truth to more people—more depth of information, more global perspective, more unbiased opinion from dispassionate observers. But this is all a smokescreen. What the Web 2.0 revolution is really delivering is superficial observations of the world around us rather than deep analysis, shrill opinion rather than considered judgment. The information business is being transformed by the Internet into the sheer noise of a hundred million bloggers all simultaneously talking about themselves. (16)

Keen repeats several of the frequent charges against the Internet: identity theft is made easy, pornographers and gamblers thrive, personal data is vulnerable, and political and corporate interests spread propaganda. What bothers him the most, however, is how all the "free information" will eventually destroy traditional media—magazines, newspapers, recording studios, and book publishers—with their resources of writers, editors, journalists, musicians, and reporters. Amateurs, according to Keen, do not have the resources to produce in-depth reporting or great music or great books, and even if they did, how could anyone find it? The sheer number of amateurs publishing on the Web makes it next to impossible to sort the good from the bad.

Keen begins by recalling the hypothetical example that if an infinite number of monkeys were given typewriters to pound, eventually one of them will type out a masterpiece. He writes, "today's amateur monkeys can use their networked computers to publish everything from uninformed political commentary, to unseemly home videos, to embarrassingly amateurish music, to unreadable poems, reviews, essays and novels" (3).

Keen's comparison of bloggers to millions of monkeys with typewriters drew the ire of bloggers even before the book appeared. Lawrence Lessig wrote in his blog (www.lessig.org/blog/) in May 2007 that Keen's book is no more reliable than the typical blog. Lessig goes after Keen's evidence:

> [W]hat is puzzling about this book is that it purports to be a book attacking the sloppiness, error and ignorance of the Internet, yet it itself is shot through with sloppiness, error and ignorance. It tells us that without institutions, and standards, to signal what we can trust (like the institution, Doubleday, that decided to print his book), we won't know what's true and what's false. But the book itself is riddled with falsity—from simple errors of fact, to gross misreadings of arguments, to the most basic errors of economics.

If an edited book from a major publisher contains errors and misreadings, Lessig contends, it undermines Keen's claim that experts save us from these inaccuracies.

The Web 2.0 debate is a series of rebuttal arguments in which the debaters attempt to knock the evidence out from under the competing claims.

Counterargument

Another way to rebut is to counterargue. In a counterargument, you do not really show the shortcomings of your opponent's point of view; you may not refer to the details of the other argument at all. Rather, you offer an argument of another point of view in the hope that it will outweigh the argument that is being rebutted. A counterarguer, in effect, says, "I hear your argument. But there is more to it than that. Now listen while I explain why another position is stronger."

The counterarguer depends on the wisdom of her or his audience members to hear all sides of an issue and to make up their minds about the merits of the case. In the following short poem, Wilfred Owen, a veteran of the horrors of World War I trench warfare, offers a counterargument to those who argue that war is noble, to those who believe along with the poet Horace that "dulce et decorum est pro patria mori"— that it is sweet and fitting to die for one's country. The vast amount of destruction and enormous loss of lives that occurred during the "war to end all wars" led people to question the belief that it is always noble to die for one's country.

Dulce Et Decorum Est

Bent double, like old beggars under sacks,
Knock-kneed, coughing like hags, we cursed through sludge,
Till on the haunting flares we turned our backs
And towards our distant rest began to trudge.
Men marched asleep. Many had lost their boots
But limped on, blood-shod. All went lame; all blind;
Drunk with fatigue; deaf even to the hoots
Of disappointed shells that dropped behind.

Gas! Gas! Quick, boys!—An ecstasy of fumbling,
Fitting the clumsy helmets just in time;
But someone still was yelling out and stumbling
And floundering like a man in fire or lime.—
Dim, through the misty panes and thick green light
As under a green sea, I saw him drowning.
In all my dreams, before my helpless sight,
He plunges at me, guttering, choking, drowning.

If in some smothering dreams you too could pace
Behind the wagon that we flung him in,
And watch the white eyes writhing in his face,
His hanging face, like a devil's sick of sin;
If you could hear, at every jolt, the blood
Come gargling from the froth-corrupted lungs,
Obscene as cancer, bitter as the cud
Of vile, incurable sores on innocent tongues,—
My friend, you would not tell with such high zest
To children ardent for some desperate glory,
The old Lie: Dulce et decorum est
Pro patria mori.

Owen does not summarize the argument in favor of being willing
to die for one's country and then refute that argument premise by
premise. Rather, his poem presents an opposing argument, supported
by a narrative of the speaker's experience in a poison-gas attack, that he
hopes will more than counterbalance what he calls "the old lie." Owen

simply ignores the good reasons that people give for being willing to die for one's country and argues instead that there are also good reasons not to do so. And he hopes that the evidence that he summons for his countering position will outweigh for his audience ("My friend") the evidence in support of the other side.

Rebuttal arguments frequently offer both refutation and counterargument. In short, people who write rebuttals work like attorneys do in a trial: they make their own cases with good reasons and hard evidence, but they also do what they can to undermine their opponent's argument. In the end the jury, the audience, decides.

Build a Rebuttal Argument

Rebuttal arguments begin with critical interrogations of the evidence underlying claims. In the era of the Internet, many writers use what turns up on the first page of a Google search. Google reports the most popular sites, however, not the most accurate ones. Mistakes and outright falsehoods are repeated because many writers on the Internet do not check their facts.

Look up a writer's sources to judge the quality of the evidence. Also, check if the writer is reporting sources accurately. Do your own fact checking. Having access to your library's databases gives you a great advantage because database sources are usually more reliable than the information you can find on the Internet.

Treat facts like a detective would. Sometimes there are alternative explanations. For example, arguments that schools are getting worse and students are getting dumber often use standardized test scores as evidence. On close inspection, however, you will find that writers often use these test scores selectively, quoting some scores and ignoring others that don't support their arguments. Furthermore, writers who quote test scores rarely take into account the population of test takers, which seldom remains constant from year to year.

When you write a counterargument with the goal of convincing readers that you have the stronger argument, your readers will appreciate your being fair about other arguments. Remember that you don't have to demolish the other person's argument, just establish that yours is better. Often you can be convincing by showing that you have thought about an issue in more depth and have taken into account more of its complexity.

WRITE A REBUTTAL ARGUMENT

Step 1 Identify an argument to argue against, as well as the argument's main claim(s)

- What exactly are you arguing against?
- Are there secondary claims attached to the main claim?
- Include a fair summary of your opponent's position in your finished rebuttal.

Examples

- Arguing against raising taxes for the purpose of building a new sports stadium (examine how proponents claim that a new sports facility will benefit the local economy).
- Arguing for raising the minimum wage (examine how opponents claim that a higher minimum wage isn't necessary and negatively affects small-business owners).

Step 2 Examine the facts on which the claim is based

- Are the facts accurate and current?
- Is there another body of facts that you can present as counterevidence?
- If the author uses statistics, can the statistics be interpreted differently?
- If the author quotes from sources, how reliable are those sources?
- Are the sources treated fairly, or are quotations taken out of context?

Step 3 Examine the assumptions on which the claim is based

- What are the primary and secondary assumptions of the claim you are rejecting?
- How are those assumptions flawed?
- Does the author resort to name-calling, use faulty reasoning, or ignore key facts?

Step 4 Analyze your potential readers

- To what extent do your potential readers support the claim that you are rejecting?
- If they strongly support that claim, how might you appeal to them to change their minds?
- What common assumptions and beliefs do you share with them?

Step 5 Write a draft

Introduction
- Provide background if the issue is unfamiliar to most of your readers.
- Give a quick summary of the competing positions even if the issue is familiar to your readers.
- Make your aim clear in your thesis statement.

Body
- Challenge the facts in the argument you are rejecting.
- Question how statistical evidence is presented and interpreted.
- Challenge the credibility of sources and authorities cited.
- Present counterevidence and countertestimony.

Conclusion
- Conclude on a firm note by underscoring your objections.
- Consider ending with a counterproposal.

Step 6 Revise, edit, proofread
- For detailed instructions, see Chapter 7.
- For a checklist to use to evaluate your draft, see pages 180–182.

PROPOSAL ARGUMENTS

Proposal arguments make the case that someone should do something: "The federal government should raise grazing fees on public lands." "The student union should renovate the old swimming pool in Butler Gymnasium." "All parents should secure their children in booster seats when driving, even for short distances." Proposals can also argue that something should *not* be done, or that people should stop doing something: "The plan to extend Highway 45 is a waste of tax dollars and citizens should not vote for it." "Don't drink and drive."

The challenge for writers of proposal arguments is to convince readers to take action. It's easy for readers to agree that something should be done, as long as they don't have to do it. It's much harder to get readers involved with the situation or convince them to spend their time or money trying to carry out the proposal. A successful proposal argument conveys a sense of urgency to motivate readers and describes definite actions they should take.

Understand How Proposal Arguments Work

Proposal arguments call for some action to be taken (or not to be taken). If readers are convinced that the proposal serves their interests, they will take action. Proposal arguments take this form:

SOMEONE should (or should not) do SOMETHING because _____ .

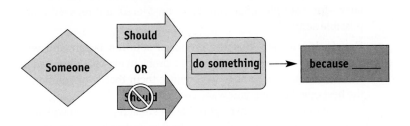

Example

We should convert existing train tracks in the downtown area to a light-rail system and build a new freight track around the city *because we need to relieve traffic and parking congestion downtown.*

Recognize Components of Proposal Arguments

Proposal arguments are often complex and involve the kinds of arguments that are discussed earlier in this chapter. Successful proposals have four major components:

- **Identifying the problem.** Sometimes, problems are evident to your intended readers. If your city is constantly tearing up the streets and then leaving them for months without doing anything to repair them, then you shouldn't have to spend much time convincing the citizens of your city that streets should be repaired more quickly. But if you raise a problem that will be unfamiliar to most of your readers, first you will have to argue that the problem exists. You also will have to define the scope of the problem. Some of the bad roads in your city might be the responsibility of the state, not the city, government.

- **Stating a proposed solution.** A strong proposal offers a clear, definite statement of exactly what you are proposing. Vague statements that "Something must be done!" may get readers stirred up about the issue, but are unlikely to lead to constructive action. A detailed proposal also adds credibility to your argument, showing that you are concerned enough to think through the nuts and bolts of the changes to be made. You can state your proposed solution near the beginning of your argument, or introduce it later—for example, after you have considered and rejected other possible solutions.

- **Convincing readers that the proposed solution is fair and will work.** Once your readers agree that a problem exists and a solution should be found, you have to convince them that your solution is the best one. Perhaps you want your city to fire the planning committee members who are responsible for street repair. You will need to show that those officials are indeed responsible for the delays, and that, once they are fired, the city will be able to quickly hire new, more effective planners.

- **Demonstrating that the solution is feasible.** Your solution not only has to work; it must be feasible, or practical, to implement. You might be able to raise money for street repairs by billing property owners for repairs to the streets in front of their houses, but opposition to such a proposal would be fierce. Most Americans will object to making individuals responsible for road repair costs when roads are used by all drivers.

You may also have to show how your proposal is better than other possible actions that could be taken. Perhaps others believe your city should hire private contractors to repair the streets more quickly, or reward work crews who finish quickly with extra pay or days off. If there are multiple proposed solutions, all perceived as equally good, then there is no clear course of action for your audience to work for. Very often, that means nothing will happen.

BUILD A PROPOSAL ARGUMENT

At this moment, you might not think that you feel strongly enough about anything to write a proposal argument. But if you write a list of things that make you mad or at least a little annoyed, then you have a start toward writing a proposal argument. Some things on your list are not going to produce proposal arguments that many people would want to read. If your roommate is a slob, you might be able to write a proposal for that person to start cleaning up more, but who else would be interested? Similarly, it might be annoying to you that where you live is too far from the ocean, but it is hard to imagine making a serious proposal to move your city closer to the coast. Short of those extremes, however, are many things that might make you think, "Why hasn't someone done something about this?" If you believe that others have something to gain if a problem is solved, or at least that the situation can be made a little better, then you might be able to develop a good proposal argument.

For instance, suppose you are living off campus, and you buy a student parking sticker when you register for courses so that you can park in the student lot. However, you quickly find out that there are too many cars and trucks for the number of available spaces, and unless you get to campus by 8:00 a.m., you aren't going to find a place to park in your assigned lot. The situation makes you angry because you believe that if you pay for a sticker, you should have a reasonable chance of finding a place to park. You see that there are unfilled lots reserved for faculty and staff next to the student parking lot, and you wonder why more spaces aren't allotted to students. You decide to write to the president of your college. You want her to direct parking and traffic services to give more spaces to students or else to build a parking garage that will accommodate more vehicles.

When you start talking to other students on campus, however, you begin to realize that the problem may be more complex than your first view of it. Your college has taken the position that if fewer students drive to campus, there will be less traffic on and around your campus. The administration wants more students to ride shuttle buses, to form car pools, or to bicycle to campus instead of driving alone. You also find out that faculty and staff members pay ten times as much as students for their parking permits, so they pay a very high premium for a guaranteed space—much too high for most students. If the president of your college is your primary audience, you first have to argue that a problem really exists. You have to convince the president that many students have no choice but to drive if they are to attend classes. You, for example, are willing to ride the shuttle buses, but they don't run often enough for you to make your classes, get back to your car that you left at home, and then drive to your job.

Next, you have to argue that your solution will solve the problem. An eightstory parking garage might be adequate to park all the cars of students who want to drive, but parking garages are very expensive to build. Even if a parking garage is the best solution, the question remains: who is going to pay for it? Many problems in life could be solved if you had access to unlimited resources, but very few people— or organizations—have such resources at their command. It's not enough to propose a solution that can resolve the problem. You have to be able to argue for the feasibility of your solution. If you want to argue that a parking garage is the solution to the parking problem on your campus, then you must also propose how to finance the garage.

SAMPLE STUDENT PROPOSAL ARGUMENT

Kim Lee

Professor Patel

RHE 306

10 May 2012

Let's Make It a Real Melting Pot with Presidential
Hopes for All

The image the United States likes to advertise is a
country that embraces diversity and creates a land of equal
opportunity for all. As the Statue of Liberty cries out,
"give me your tired, your poor, your huddled masses yearn-
ing to breathe free," American politicians gleefully evoke
such images to frame the United States as a bastion for all
things good, fair, and equal. As a proud American, however, I must nonetheless highlight one of the cracks in this
façade of equality. Imagine that a couple decides to adopt
an orphaned child from China. They follow all of the legal
processes deemed necessary by both countries. They fly
abroad and bring home their (once parentless) six-month-
old baby boy. They raise and nurture him, and while teaching him to embrace his ethnicity, they also teach him to
love Cap'n Crunch, baseball, and *Sesame Street*. He grows
and eventually attends an ethnically diverse American
public school. One day his fifth-grade teacher tells the class
that anyone can grow up to be president. To clarify her
point, she turns to the boy, knowing his background, and
states, "No, you could not be president, Stu, but you could
still be a senator. That's something to aspire to!" How do
Stu's parents explain this rule to this American-raised child?
This scenario will become increasingly common, yet as the

Lee 2

Constitution currently reads, only "natural-born" citizens
may run for the offices of president and vice president.
Neither these children nor the thousands of hardworking
Americans who chose to make America their official home-
land may aspire to the highest political position in the land.
While the huddled masses may enter, it appears they must
retain a second-class citizen ranking.

The issue arose most recently when bloggers, media
personalities, and some elected officials alleged that Barack
Obama was born in Kenya, not Hawaii, and that his birth
certificate is a forgery. The release of a certified copy of
Obama's Certificate of Live Birth (the "long form") and
other evidence including birth announcements in two Hawaii
newspapers in August 1961 answered Donald Trump and
other prominent "birthers" (Shear). Lost in the controversy
was the question: Should it matter where Obama or any
other candidate was born? In a land where everyone but
American Indians are immigrants or descendants of immigrants, why should being born in the United States be considered an essential qualification for election as President?

The provision arose from very different circumstances
than those of today. The "natural-born" stipulation regarding the presidency stems from the self-same meeting
of minds that brought the American people the Electoral
College. During the Constitutional Convention of 1787, the
Congress formulated the regulatory measures associated
with the office of the president. A letter sent from John Jay
to George Washington during this period reads as follows:

"Permit me to hint," Jay wrote, "whether it would
not be wise and seasonable to provide a strong check
to the admission of foreigners into the administration

of our national government; and to declare expressly that the Commander in Chief of the American army shall not be given to, nor devolve on, any but a natural-born citizen." (Mathews A1)

Shortly thereafter, Article II, Section I, Clause V, of the Constitution declared that "No Person except a natural born Citizen, or a Citizen of the United States at the time of the Adoption of this Constitution, shall be eligible to the Office of President." Jill A. Pryor states in the *Yale Law Journal* that "some writers have suggested that Jay was responding to rumors that foreign princes might be asked to assume the presidency" (881). Many cite disastrous examples of foreign rule in the eighteenth century as the impetus for the "natural-born" clause. For example, in 1772—only 15 years prior to the adoption of the statute—Poland had been divided up by Prussia, Russia, and Austria (Kasindorf). Perhaps an element of self-preservation and not ethnocentrism led to the questionable stipulation. Nonetheless, in the twenty-first century this clause reeks of xenophobia.

The Fourteenth Amendment clarified the difference between "naturalborn" and "native-born" citizens by spelling out the citizenship status of children born to American parents outside of the United States (Ginsberg 929). This clause qualifies individuals such as Senator John McCain—born in Panama—for presidency. This change, however, is not adequate. I propose that the United States abolish the natural-born clause and replace it with a stipulation that allows naturalized citizens to run for president. This amendment would state that a candidate must have been naturalized and must have lived in residence in the United States for a period of at least twenty-five years. The present

Lee 4

time is ideal for this change. This amendment could simultaneously honor the spirit of the Constitution, protect and ensure the interests of the United States, promote an international image of inclusiveness, and grant heretofore-withheld rights to thousands of legal and loyal United States citizens.

In our push for change, we must make clear the importance of this amendment. It would not provide special rights for would-be terrorists. To the contrary, it would fulfill the longtime promises of the nation. Naturalized citizens have been contributing to the United States for centuries. Many nameless Mexican, Irish, and Asian Americans sweated and toiled to build the American railroads. The public has welcomed naturalized Americans such as Bob Hope, Albert Pujols, and Peter Jennings into their hearts and living rooms. Individuals such as German-born Henry Kissinger and Czechoslovakian-born Madeleine Albright have held high posts in the American government and have served as respected aides to its presidents. The amendment must make clear that it is not about one man's celebrity. Approximately seven hundred foreign-born Americans have won the Medal of Honor, and over sixty thousand proudly serve in the United States military today (Siskind 5). The "natural-born" clause must be removed to provide each of these people—over half a million naturalized in 2003 alone—with equal footing to those who were born into citizenship rather than working for it (United States).

Since the passing of the Bill of Rights, only 17 amendments have been ratified. This process takes time and overwhelming congressional and statewide support. To alter the Constitution, a proposed amendment must pass

Lee 5

with a two-thirds "supermajority" in both the House of Representatives and the Senate. In addition, the proposal must find favor in two-thirds of the 50 state legislatures. In short, this task will not be easy. In order for this change to occur, a grassroots campaign must work to dispel misinformation regarding naturalized citizens and to force the hands of senators and representatives wishing to retain their congressional seats. We must take this proposal to ethnicity-specific political groups from both sides of the aisle, business organizations, and community activist groups. We must convince representatives that this issue matters. Only through raising voices and casting votes can the people enact change. Only then can every American child see the possibility for limitless achievement and equality. Only then can everyone find the same sense of pride in the possibility for true American diversity in the highest office in the land.

Lee 6

Works Cited

Epstein, Edward. "Doubt about a Foreign-Born
    President." *San Francisco Chronicle* 6 Oct. 2004: A5.
    LexisNexis Academic. Web. 16 Apr. 2012.
Ginsberg, Gordon. "Citizenship: Expatriation: Distinction
    between Naturalized and Natural Born Citizens."
    Michigan Law Review 50 (1952): 926–29. *JSTOR*.
    Web. 16 Apr. 2012.

Lee 7

Kasindorf, Martin. "Should the Constitution Be Amended for Arnold?" *USA Today* 2 Dec. 2004. *LexisNexis Academic.* Web. 18 Apr. 2012.

Mathews, Joe. "Maybe Anyone Can Be President." *Los Angeles Times* 2 Feb. 2005: A1. *LexisNexis Academic.* Web. 16 Apr. 2012.

Pryor, Jill A. "The Natural Born Citizen Clause and Presidential Eligibility: An Approach for Resolving Two Hundred Years of Uncertainty." *Yale Law Journal* 97.5 (1988): 881–99. Print.

Shear, Michael D. "With Document, Obama Seeks to End 'Birther' Issue." *New York Times.* New York Times, 27 Apr. 2011. Web. 28 Apr. 2012.

Siskind, Lawrence J. "Why Shouldn't Arnold Run?" *Recorder* 10 Dec. 2004: 5. *LexisNexis Academic.* Web. 10 Apr. 2012.

United States. Dept. of Commerce. Census Bureau. "The Fourth of July 2005." *Facts for Features.* U.S. Dept. of Commerce, 27 June 2005. Web. 17 Apr. 2012.

WRITE A PROPOSAL ARGUMENT

Step 1 Make a claim

Make a proposal claim advocating a specific change or course of action.

Template
- We should (or should not) do SOMETHING.

Examples

In an essay of five or fewer pages, it's difficult to propose solutions to big problems such as persistent poverty. Proposals that address local problems are more manageable, and sometimes they get actual results.

- Redesigning the process of registering for courses, applying for financial aid, or making appointments to be more efficient.
- Creating bicycle lanes to make cycling safer and to reduce traffic.
- Streamlining the rules for recycling newspapers, bottles, and cans to encourage increased participation.

Step 2 Identify the problem

- What exactly is the problem?
- Who is most affected by the problem?
- Has anyone tried to do anything about it? If so, why haven't they succeeded?
- What is likely to happen in the future if the problem isn't solved?

Step 3 Propose your solution

- State your solution as specifically as you can.
- What exactly do you want to achieve?
- How exactly will your solution work?
- Can it be accomplished quickly, or will it have to be phased in over a few years?
- Has anything like it been tried elsewhere? If so, what happened?

Step 4 Consider other solutions

- What other solutions have been or might be proposed for this problem, including doing nothing?
- Why is your solution better?

Step 5 Examine the feasibility of your solution

- How easy is your solution to implement?
- Will the people most affected by your solution be willing to go along with it? (For example, lots of things can be accomplished if enough people volunteer, but groups often have difficulty getting enough volunteers to work without pay.)
- If your solution costs money, how do you propose to pay for it?
- Who is most likely to reject your proposal because it is not practical enough?
- How can you convince your readers that your proposal can be achieved?

Step 6 Analyze your potential readers

- Whom are you writing for?
- How interested will your readers be in this problem?
- How much does this problem affect them?
- How would your solution benefit them directly and indirectly?

Step 7 Write a draft

Introduction

- Set out the issue or problem, perhaps by telling about your experience or the experience of someone you know.
- Argue for the seriousness of the problem.
- Give some background about the problem if necessary.

Body

- Present your solution. Consider setting out your solution first, explaining how it will work, discussing other possible solutions, and arguing that yours is better. Or consider discussing other possible solutions first, arguing that they don't solve the problem or are not feasible, and then presenting your solution.
- Make clear the goals of your solution. Many solutions cannot solve problems completely. If you are proposing a solution for juvenile crime in your neighborhood, for example, you cannot expect to eliminate all juvenile crime.
- Describe in detail the steps in implementing your solution and how they will solve the problem you have identified. You can impress your readers with the care with which you have thought through this problem.
- Explain the positive consequences that will follow from your proposal. What good things will happen, and what bad things will be avoided, if your advice is taken?
- Argue that your proposal is feasible and can be put into practice.

Conclusion

- Issue a call to action—if your readers agree with you, they will want to take action.
- Restate and emphasize exactly what readers need to do to solve the problem.

Step 8 Revise, edit, proofread

- For detailed instructions, see Chapter 7.
- For a checklist to use to evaluate your draft, see pages 180–182.

5

Researching an Argument

If you have an assignment that requires research, look closely at what you are being asked to do. The assignment may ask you to define, evaluate, analyze causes, rebut another's argument, or propose a course of action. You may be writing for experts, for students like yourself, or for the general public. The purpose of your research and your potential audience will help guide your strategies for research.

The key is understanding what is expected of you. You are being asked to do the following.

1. Find a subject.
2. Ask a question about the subject.
3. Find out what has been said about this subject.
4. Make a contribution to the discussion about this subject.

Give yourself enough time to do a thorough job. As you conduct your research, expect to focus better on your subject, to find a few dead ends, and to spend more time on the project than you initially thought. Remember the first principle of doing research: things take longer than you think they will.

FIND A SUBJECT

One good way to begin is by browsing, which may also show you the breadth of possibilities included in a topic and possibly lead you to new topics.

You might begin browsing by doing one or more of the following.

- **Visit "Research by Subject" on your library's Web site.** Clicking on a subject such as "African and African American Studies" will take you to a list of online resources. Often you can find an e-mail link to a reference librarian who can assist you.

- **Look for topics in your courses.** Browse your course notes and readings. Are there any topics you might want to explore in greater depth?

- **Browse a Web subject directory.** Web subject directories, including Yahoo Directory (dir.yahoo.com), are useful when you want to narrow a topic or learn what subcategories a topic might contain. In addition to the Web subject directories, your library's Web site may have a link to the *Opposing Viewpoints* database.

- **Look for topics as you read.** When you read actively, you ask questions and respond to ideas in the text. Review what you wrote in the margins or the notes you have made about something you read that interested you. You may find a potential topic.

ASK A RESEARCH QUESTION AND GATHER INFORMATION

Often you'll be surprised by the amount of information your initial browsing uncovers. Your next task will be to identify a question for your research project within that mass of information. This **researchable question** will be the focus of the remainder of your research and ultimately of your research project or paper. Browsing on the subject of organic foods, for example, might lead you to one of the following researchable questions.

- How do farmers benefit from growing organic produce?

- Why are organic products more expensive than non-organic products?

- Are Americans being persuaded to buy more organic products?

Once you have formulated a research question, you should begin thinking about what kind of research you will need to do to address the question.

Find Information About the Subject

Most researchers rely partly or exclusively on the work of others as sources of information. Research based on the work of others is called **secondary research**. In the past this information was contained almost exclusively in collections of print materials housed in libraries, but today enormous amounts of information are available through library databases and on the Web.

Much of the research done at a university creates new information through **primary research**—such as experiments and examination of historical documents—and **field research**, including data-gathering surveys, interviews, and detailed observations. Sometimes you may be researching a question that requires you to gather firsthand information with field research. For example, if you are researching a campus issue such as the impact of a new library fee on students' budgets, you may need to conduct interviews, make observations, and give a survey.

Interviews

College campuses are a rich source of experts in many areas, including people on the faculty and in the surrounding community. Interviewing experts on your research subject can help build your knowledge base. You can use interviews to discover what the people most affected by a particular issue are thinking, such as why students object to some fees and not others.

- Decide what you want or need to know and who best can provide that for you.

- Schedule each interview in advance, and let the person know why you are conducting the interview. Estimate how long your interview will take, and tell your subject how much of his or her time you will need.

- Plan your questions in advance. Write down a few questions and have a few more in mind.

- If you want to record the interview, ask for permission in advance. A recording device sometimes can intimidate the person you are interviewing.

- When you are finished, thank your subject, and ask his or her permission to get in touch again if you have additional questions.

Surveys

Extensive surveys that can be projected to large populations, like the ones used in political polls, require the effort of many people. Small surveys, however, often can provide insight on local issues, such as what percentage of students might be affected if library hours were reduced.

- Decide on who you need to survey and how many respondents your survey will require.

- Write a few specific, unambiguous questions. People will fill out your survey quickly, and if the questions are confusing, the results will be meaningless.

- Include one or two open-ended questions, such as "What do you like about X?" or "What don't you like about X?" Open-ended questions can be difficult to interpret, but sometimes they turn up information you had not anticipated.

- Test the questions on a few people before you conduct the survey.

- Think about how you will interpret your survey. Multiple-choice formats make data easy to tabulate, but often they miss key information. Open-ended questions will require you to figure out a way to sort responses into categories.

Observations

Observing can be a valuable source of data. For example, if you are researching why a particular office on your campus does not operate efficiently, observe what happens when students enter and how the staff responds to their presence.

- Choose a place where you can observe with the least intrusion. The less people wonder about what you are doing, the better.

- Carry a tablet, laptop, or paper notebook and write extensive field notes. Record as much information as you can, and worry about analyzing it later.

- Record the date, exactly where you were, exactly when you arrived and left, and important details like the number of people present.
- Find a quiet time shortly after you observe to analyze your data and note the key observations.

DRAFT A WORKING THESIS

Once you have done some preliminary research into your question, you can begin to craft a working thesis. Perhaps you have found a lot of interesting material about the increasing popularity of organic products, including meat, dairy products, and produce. You have discovered that due to this trend, large corporations such as Walmart are beginning to offer organic products in their stores. However, the enormous demand for organic products that this creates is endangering smaller organic farmers and producers. As you research the question of why small farmers and producers in the United States are endangered and what small farmers and producers in other countries have done to protect themselves, a working thesis begins to emerge.

Write your subject, research question, and working thesis on a note card or sheet of paper. Keep your working thesis handy. You may need to revise it several times until the wording is precise. As you research, ask yourself, does this information tend to support my thesis? Information that does not support your thesis is still important! It may lead you to adjust your thesis or even to abandon it altogether. You may need to find another source or reason that shows your thesis is still valid.

SUBJECT: Increased demand for organic products endangering smaller farmers and producers

RESEARCH QUESTION: How can smaller organic farms and producers protect themselves from becoming extinct?

(Continued on next page)

WORKING THESIS: In order to meet the increasing demand for organic products that has been created by larger corporations such as Walmart, smaller organic farmers and producers should form regional co-ops. These co-ops will work together to supply regional chains, much as co-ops of small farmers and dairies in Europe work together, thereby cutting transportation and labor costs and ensuring their survival in a much-expanded market.

FIND SOURCES

The distinction between doing research online and in the library is blurring as more and more libraries put their collections online. Many colleges and universities have made most of the major resources in their reference rooms available online. Still, your library is usually the best place to begin any research project because it contains some materials that are not available anywhere else. Moreover, professional librarians will help you locate sources quickly so you get the most out of your research time.

Search with Keywords

For most research projects, you will begin with a subject search using one or more **keywords** or search terms that describe the subject. Entries for subjects in your library's online catalog and in databases will help you find keywords. If you find a book or article that is about your exact topic, use the subject terms to locate additional items. The sample below, for a book from an online catalog, shows the keywords under *subjects*. Try entering the subject terms individually and in combination in new subject searches to find more items similar to this one.

AUTHOR:

Solove, Daniel J., 1972-

TITLE:

The digital person: technology and privacy in the information age/Daniel J. Solove.

PUBLISHED:

New York: New York University Press, c2004.

SUBJECTS:

Data protection—Law and legislation—United States.
Electronic records—Access control—United States.
Public records—Law and legislation—United States.
Government information—United States.
Privacy, Right of—United States.

The simplest keyword searches return the most results, but often they are not the results you need. For example, imagine typing the word *capitalism* into the keyword search window on your library's online catalog and getting several thousand results, including subjects such as radicals and capitalism, global capitalism, American capitalism, new capitalism, women and capitalism, socialism and capitalism, slavery and capitalism, ethics and capitalism, and so on.

If you want to focus on how capitalism affects the natural world, however, then you can narrow your search using two or more keywords. For example, if you use the terms *capitalism* and *ecology* in the search window, you would likely receive a more manageable 25 or so results. You could then read through the titles and perhaps the brief abstracts provided and decide that a book such as *Wild Capitalism: Environmental Activists and Post-Socialist Political Ecology in Hungary* may not be as useful to you as a book titled *Ecology Against Capitalism*.

You can further limit your search by specifying what you don't want by using NOT. For example, if you are interested in air pollution control policies, but not those used in California, you would type *air pollution control policies* NOT *California.*

Find Sources in Databases

Sources found through library **databases** have already been filtered for you by professional librarians. They will include some common sources like popular magazines and newspapers, but the greatest value of database sources are the many journals, abstracts, studies, e-books, and other writing produced by specialists whose work has been scrutinized and commented on by other experts. When you read a source from a library database, chances are you are hearing an informed voice in an important debate.

Locate Databases

You can find databases on your library's Web site. Sometimes you will find a list of databases. Sometimes you select a subject, and then you are directed to databases. Sometimes you select the name of a database vendor such as EBSCO or ProQuest. The vendor is the company that provides databases to the library.

Use Databases

Your library has a list of databases and indexes by subject. If you can't find this list on your library's Web site, ask a **reference librarian** for help. Follow these steps to find articles.

1. Select a database appropriate to your subject or a comprehensive database like *Academic Search Complete, Academic Search Premier,* or *LexisNexis Academic.*

2. Search the database using your list of keywords.

3. Once you have chosen an article, print or e-mail to yourself the complete citation to the article. Look for the e-mail link after you click on the item you want.

4. Print or e-mail to yourself the full text if it is available. The full text is better than cutting and pasting because you might

lose track of which words are yours, leading to unintended plagiarism.

5. If the full text is not available, check the online library catalog to see if your library has the journal.

Your library will probably have printed handouts or information on the Web that tells you which database to use for a particular subject. Ask a librarian who works at the reference or information desk to help you.

If you wish to get only full-text articles, you can check that option. Full-text documents give you the same text you would find in print. Sometimes the images are not reproduced in the HTML versions, but the PDF versions show the actual printed copy. Get the PDF version if it is available. Articles in HTML format usually do not contain the page numbers.

COMMON DATABASES

Academic OneFile	Indexes periodicals from the arts, humanities, sciences, social sciences, and general news, with full-text articles and images. (Formerly *Expanded Academic ASAP*).
Academic Search Premier and Complete	Provides full-text articles for thousands of scholarly publications, including social sciences, humanities, education, computer sciences, engineering, language and linguistics, literature, medical sciences, and ethnic-studies journals.
ArticleFirst	Indexes journals in business, the humanities, medicine, science, and social sciences.
EBSCOhost Research Databases	Gateway to a large collection of EBSCO databases, including *Academic Search Premier and Complete, Business Source Premier and Complete, ERIC*, and *Medline*.
Factiva	Provides full-text articles on business topics, including articles from the *Wall Street Journal*.

(Continued on next page)

Google Books	Allows you to search within books and gives you snippets surrounding search terms for copyrighted books. Many books out of copyright have the full text. Available for everyone.
Google Scholar	Searches scholarly literature according to criteria of relevance. Available for everyone.
General OneFile	Contains millions of full-text articles about a wide range of academic and general-interest topics.
LexisNexis Academic	Provides full text of a wide range of newspapers, magazines, government and legal documents, and company profiles from around the world.
Opposing Viewpoints Resource Center	Provides full-text articles representing differing points of view on current issues.
ProQuest Databases	Like EBSCOhost, ProQuest is a gateway to a large collection of databases with over 100 billion pages, including the best archives of doctoral dissertations and historical newspapers.

Find Sources on the Web

You likely use the Web regularly to find information about products, restaurants, stores, services, jobs, people, maps, hobbies, music, films, and other entertainment. But researching an academic paper on the Web is different from such everyday tasks. The Web can be a powerful tool for research, but it also has many traps for the unwary.

Because anyone can publish on the Web, there is no overall quality control and there are no systems of organization as there are in a library. Nevertheless, the Web offers you some resources for current topics that would be difficult to find in a library. The keys to success are knowing where you are most likely to find current and accurate information about the particular question you are researching, and knowing how to access that information.

Use Search Engines

Search engines designed for the Web work in ways similar to library databases and your library's online catalog, but with one major difference. Databases typically do some screening of the items they list, but search engines potentially take you to every Web site that isn't password protected—millions of pages in all. Consequently, you have to work harder to limit searches on the Web or you can be deluged with tens of thousands of items.

Search engines often produce too many hits and are therefore not always useful. If you look only at the first few items, you may miss what is most valuable. The alternative is to refine your search. Most search engines offer you the option of an advanced search, which gives you the opportunity to limit numbers.

Find Discussion Forums, Groups, Blogs, Wikis, Podcasts, and Online Video

Discussion forums and **discussion groups** are Internet sites for people to discuss thousands of specific topics. The Groups section of Google (groups.google.com) has an archive of several hundred million messages that can be searched. Much of the conversation on these sites is undocumented and highly opinionated, but you can still gather important information about people's attitudes and get tips about other sources, which you can verify later.

Web logs, better known as **blogs**, also are sources of public opinion. Several tools have been developed recently to search blogs: Bloglines, Google Blog Search, Technorati, and IceRocket. Blogs are not screened and are not considered authoritative sources, but blogs can sometimes lead you to quality sources.

Wikis are Web applications designed to let multiple authors write, edit, and review content. The best-known wiki is Wikipedia (www.wikipedia.org), a controversial online encyclopedia where any visitor can change an entry. Wikipedia can provide a useful introduction to many popular-culture topics, but do not rely on Wikipedia to be completely accurate. Many individual professors and teachers, as well as some colleges and universities, forbid the use of Wikipedia as a source in academic papers.

Podcasts are digital media files available on the Internet for playback on portable media players. Many of these files are news, opinion, and entertainment broadcasts from major media outlets such as NPR (www.npr.org/rss/podcast/podcast_directory.php). Individuals can also create and distribute files for podcasts. Information from these podcasts should be treated with the same critical eye (and ear!) you use for blogs and personal Web pages.

Similarly, sites that offer **streaming video** such as YouTube (www.youtube.com) and Google Video (www.videogoogle.com) can be used to access videos from reputable sources, such as interviews and newscasts as well as eyewitness footage of events or situations around the world. Most videos on these sites, however, were created strictly for entertainment purposes.

Find Print Sources

Print sources may seem "old fashioned" if you grew up with the Internet. You might even feel a little bit intimidated by them. But they are the starting point for much of the research done by experts. In college and beyond, they are indispensable. No matter how current the topic you are researching, you will likely find information in print sources that is simply not available online.

Print sources have other advantages as well.

- Books are shelved according to subject, allowing easy browsing.
- Books often have bibliographies, directing you to other research on the subject.
- You can search for books in multiple ways: author, title, subject, or call letter.
- The majority of print sources have been evaluated by scholars, editors, and publishers, who decided whether they merited publication.

Find Books

Nearly all libraries now shelve books according to the Library of Congress Classification System, which uses a combination of letters and numbers to give you the book's unique location in the library. The Library of Congress call number begins with a letter or letters that represent the broad subject area into which the book is classified.

Locating Books in Your Library

The floors of your library where books are shelved are referred to as the stacks. The call number will enable you to find the item in the stacks. You will need to consult the locations guide for your library, which gives the level and section where an item is shelved.

Locating e-Books

Use your library's online catalog to find e-books the same way you find printed books. You'll see on the record "e-book" or "electronic resource." Click on the link and you can read the book and often download a few pages.

Find Journal Articles

Like books, **scholarly journals** provide in-depth examinations of subjects. The articles in scholarly journals are written by experts, and they usually contain lists of references that can guide you to other research on a subject.

Popular journals are useful for gaining general information. Articles in popular magazines are usually short with few, if any, source references and are typically written by journalists. Some instructors frown on using popular magazines, but these journals can be valuable for researching current opinion on a particular topic.

Many scholarly journals and popular magazines are available on your library's Web site. Find them the same way you look for books, using your library's online catalog. Databases increasingly contain the full text of articles, allowing you to read and copy the contents onto your computer. If the article you are looking for isn't available online, the paper copy will be shelved with the books in your library.

EVALUATE SOURCES

A successful search for sources will turn up many more items than you can use in your final product. You have to make decisions about what is important and relevant. Return to your research question and working thesis to determine which items are relevant and useful to your project.

Evaluate Print and Database Sources

How reliable are your sources? Books are expensive to print and distribute, so book publishers generally protect their investment by providing some level of editorial oversight. Print and database sources in libraries have an additional layer of oversight because someone has decided that a book or journal is worth purchasing and cataloging. Web sites, in contrast, can be put up and changed quickly, so information can be—and often is—posted thoughtlessly.

But print sources contain their share of biased, inaccurate, and misleading information. Over the years librarians have developed a set of criteria for evaluating print sources. These criteria are summarized in the box below.

EVALUATING PRINT SOURCES

Source	Who published the book or article? Scholarly books and articles in scholarly journals are reviewed by experts in the field before they are published. They are generally more reliable than popular magazines and books, which tend to emphasize what is entertaining at the expense of comprehensiveness.
Author	Who wrote the book or article? What are the author's qualifications?
Timeliness	How current is the source? If you are researching a fast-developing subject such as vaccines for Asian bird flu, then currency is very important. Currency might not be as important for a historical subject, but even historical figures and events are often reinterpreted.
Evidence	Where does the evidence come from—facts, interviews, observations, surveys, or experiments? Is the evidence adequate to support the author's claims?
Biases	Can you detect particular biases of the author? How do the author's biases affect the interpretation offered?
Advertising	Is advertising a prominent part of the journal or newspaper? How might the ads affect what gets printed?

Evaluate Web Sources

All electronic search tools share a common problem: They often give you too many sources. Web search engines pull up thousands of hits, and these hits may vary dramatically in quality. No one regulates or checks most information put on the Web, and it's no surprise that much of what is on the Web is highly opinionated or false.

Misleading Web Sites

Some Web sites are put up as jokes. Other Web sites are deliberately misleading. Many prominent Web sites draw imitators who want to cash in on the commercial visibility. The Web site for the Campaign for Tobacco-Free Kids (www.tobaccofreekids.org), for example, has an imitator (www.smokefreekids.com) that sells software for antismoking education. The *.com* URL is often a tip-off that a site's main motive is profit.

Biased Web Sites

Always approach Web sites with an eye toward evaluating their content. For example, Web sites with *.com* URLs that offer medical information often contain strong biases in addition to the motive to make money. The creators of the Web site Thinktwice.com, sponsored by the Global Vaccine Institute, oppose the vaccination of children. On the site you can find claims that the polio vaccine administered to millions of people in the United States causes cancer because it was contaminated with Simian Virus 40. Always look for additional sources for verification. The U.S. Centers for Disease Control publishes fact sheets with the latest information about diseases and their prevention, including one on the polio vaccine and Simian Virus 40.

EVALUATING WEB SOURCES

Source   Look for the site's ownership in the Web address. If a Web site doesn't indicate ownership, attempt to discover who put it up and why. The domain can offer clues: *.gov* is used by government bodies and *.edu* is used by colleges and universities. In general, *.edu* sites are more reliable than *.com* sites.

(*Continued on next page*)

Author	Often Web sites give no information about their authors other than an e-mail address, if that. In such cases it is difficult or impossible to determine the author's qualifications. Look up the author on Google. If qualifications are listed, is the author an expert in the field? Some sites, such as Wikipedia, allow anyone to add or delete information. An entry on Wikipedia can (and often does) change from day to day, depending on who has edited the entry most recently.
Timeliness	Many Web pages do not list when they were last updated; thus you cannot determine their currency. Furthermore, there are thousands of deserted ghost sites on the Web— sites that the owners have abandoned but that search engines still turn up.
Evidence	The accuracy of any evidence found on the Web is often hard to verify. The most reliable information on the Web stands up to the tests of print evaluation, with clear indication of the sponsoring organization. Any factual information should be supported by indicating its source. Reliable Web sites list their sources.
Biases	Many Web sites announce their viewpoint on controversial issues, but others conceal their attitude with a reasonable tone and seemingly factual evidence such as statistics. Citations and bibliographies do not ensure that a site is reliable. Look carefully at the links and sources cited. Are the sources reliable?
Advertising	Many Web sites are infomercials aimed at getting you to buy a product or service. While they might contain useful information, they are no more trustworthy than other forms of advertising.

Other Internet Sources

Other Internet sources, such as online newsgroups, blogs, podcasts, wikis, and online videos, can give you useful ideas but are generally not considered authoritative. If you do find facts on Wikipedia, be sure to confirm them with another source. E-mail communication from an expert in the field might be considered an authoritative source, but personal e-mails are generally not considered worthy of inclusion in a research paper. Remember that a key reason to cite sources is to allow other researchers to read and evaluate the sources you used.

6

Documenting an Argument

Writers in college are expected to provide the sources of information so that readers can consult the same sources the writer used.

AVOID PLAGIARISM

Plagiarism means claiming credit for someone else's intellectual work no matter whether it's to make money or get a better grade. Intentional or not, plagiarism has dire consequences. Reputable authors have gotten into trouble through carelessness by copying passages from published sources without acknowledging those sources. A number of famous people have had their reputations tarnished by accusations of plagiarism, and several prominent journalists have lost their jobs and careers for copying the work of other writers and passing it off as their own.

Deliberate Plagiarism

If you buy a paper on the Web, copy someone else's paper word for word, or take an article off the Web and turn it in as yours, it's plain stealing, and people who take that risk should know that the punishment can be severe—usually failure for the course and sometimes expulsion. Deliberate plagiarism is easy for your instructors to spot because they recognize shifts in style, and it is easy for them to use search engines to find the sources of work stolen from the Web.

Patch Plagiarism

The use of the Web has increased instances of plagiarism in college. Some students view the Internet as a big free buffet where they can grab anything, paste it in a file, and submit it as their own work. Other students intend to submit work that is their own, but they commit patch plagiarism because they aren't careful in taking notes to distinguish the words of others from their own words.

What You Are Not Required to Acknowledge

Fortunately, common sense governs issues of academic plagiarism. The standards of documentation are not so strict that the source of every fact you cite must be acknowledged. You do not have to document the following.

- **Facts available from many sources.** For example, many reference sources report that the death toll of the sinking of the *Titanic* on April 15, 1912, was around 1,500.

- **Results of your own field research.** If you take a survey and report the results, you don't have to cite yourself. You do need to cite individual interviews.

What You Are Required to Acknowledge

The following sources should be acknowledged with an in-text citation and an entry in the list of works cited (MLA style) or the list of references (APA style).

- **Quotations.** Short quotations should be enclosed within quotation marks, and quotations longer than four lines should be indented as a block.

- **Summaries and paraphrases.** Summaries represent the author's argument in miniature as accurately as possible. Paraphrases restate the author's argument in your own words.

- **Facts that are not common knowledge.** For facts that are not easily found in general reference works, cite the source.

- **Ideas that are not common knowledge.** The sources of theories, analyses, statements of opinion, and arguable claims should be cited.

- **Statistics, research findings, examples, graphs, charts, and illustrations.** As a reader you should be skeptical about statistics and research findings when the source is not mentioned. When a writer does not cite the sources of statistics and research findings, there is no way of knowing how reliable the sources are or whether the writer is making them up.

PLAGIARISM IN COLLEGE WRITING

If you find any of the following problems in your academic writing, you may be guilty of plagiarizing someone else's work. Because plagiarism is usually inadvertent, it is especially important that you understand what constitutes using sources responsibly. Avoid these pitfalls.

- **Missing attribution.** Make sure the author of a quotation has been identified. Include a lead-in or signal phrase that provides attribution to the source, and identify the author in the citation.

- **Missing quotation marks.** You must put quotation marks around material quoted directly from a source.

- **Inadequate citation.** Give a page number to show where in the source the quotation appears or where a paraphrase or summary is drawn from.

- **Paraphrase relies too heavily on the source.** Be careful that the wording or sentence structure of a paraphrase does not follow the source too closely.

- **Distortion of meaning.** Don't allow your paraphrase or summary to distort the meaning of the source, and don't take a quotation out of context, resulting in a change of meaning.

- **Missing works-cited entry.** The Works Cited page must include all the works cited in the project.

- **Inadequate citation of images.** A figure or photo must appear with a caption and a citation to indicate the source of the image. If material includes a summary of data from a visual source, an attribution or citation must be given for the graphic being summarized.

Avoid Plagiarism When Taking Notes

The best way to avoid unintentional plagiarism is to take care to distinguish source words from your own words. Don't mix words from the source with your own words.

- **Create a working bibliography and make separate files for content notes.** Create a file for each source and label it clearly with the author's name. If you work on paper, use a separate page for each source. At the top of each page, write down all the information you need for a list of works cited or a list of references in your working bibliography.

- **If you copy anything from a source when taking notes, place those words in quotation marks and note the page number(s) where those words appear.** If you copy words from an online source, take special care to note the source. You could easily copy online material and later not be able to find where it came from.

- **Print out the entire source so you can refer to it later.** Having photocopies or complete printed files allows you to double-check later that you haven't used words from the source by mistake and that any words you quote are accurate.

QUOTE SOURCES WITHOUT PLAGIARIZING

Effective research writing builds on the work of others. You can and should summarize or paraphrase the work of others, but often it is best to let the authors speak in your text by quoting their exact words. Indicate the words of others by placing them inside quotation marks.

Most people who get into plagiarism trouble lift words from a source and use them without quotation marks. Where the line is drawn is easiest to illustrate with an example. In the following passage, Steven Johnson takes sharp issue with the metaphor of surfing applied to the Web:

> The concept of "surfing" does a terrible injustice to what it means to navigate around the Web.... What makes the idea of cybersurf so infuriating is the implicit connection drawn to television. Web surfing, after all, is a derivation of channel surfing—the term thrust upon the world by the rise of remote controls and cable panoply in the mid-eighties....

Applied to the boob tube, of course, the term was not altogether inappropriate. Surfing at least implied that channel-hopping was more dynamic, more involved, than the old routine of passive consumption. Just as a real-world surfer's enjoyment depended on the waves delivered up by the ocean, the channel surfer was at the mercy of the programmers and network executives. The analogy took off because it worked well in the one-to-many system of cable TV, where your navigational options were limited to the available channels.

But when the term crossed over to the bustling new world of the Web, it lost a great deal of precision.... Web surfing and channel surfing are genuinely different pursuits; to imagine them as equivalents is to ignore the defining characteristics of each medium. Or at least that's what happens in theory. In practice, the Web takes on the greater burden. The television imagery casts the online surfer in the random, anesthetic shadow of TV programming, roaming from site to site like a CD player set on shuffle play. But what makes the online world so revolutionary is the fact that there *are* connections between each stop on a Web itinerant's journey. The links that join those various destinations are links of association, not randomness. A channel surfer hops back and forth between different channels because she's bored. A Web surfer clicks on a link because she's interested.

> —Steven Johnson. *Interface Culture: How New Technology Transforms the Way We Create and Communicate.* New York: Harper, 1997. 107-109. Print.

If you were writing a paper or putting up a Web site that concerns Web surfing, you might want to mention the distinction that Johnson makes between channel surfing and surfing on the Web.

Quote Directly Using Quotation Marks

If you quote directly, you must place quotation marks around all words you take from the original:

One observer marks this contrast: "A channel surfer hops back and forth between different channels because she's bored. A Web surfer clicks on a link because she's interested" (Johnson 109).

Notice that the quotation is introduced and not just dropped in. This example follows MLA style, where the citation—(Johnson 109)—goes outside the quotation marks but before the final period. In MLA style, source references are made according to the author's last name, which refers you to the full citation in the list of works cited at the end. Following the author's name is the page number where the quotation can be located. (Notice that there is no comma after the name.)

Attribute Every Quotation

If the author's name appears in the sentence, cite only the page number, in parentheses:

> According to Steven Johnson, "A channel surfer hops back and forth between different channels because she's bored. A Web surfer clicks on a link because she's interested" (109).

Quote Words That Are Quoted in Your Source with Single Quotation Marks

Use single quotation marks to quote material that is already quoted in your source:

> Steven Johnson uses the metaphor of a Gothic cathedral to describe a computer interface: "'The principle of the Gothic architecture,' Coleridge once said, 'is infinity made imaginable.' The same could be said for the modern interface" (42).

SUMMARIZE AND PARAPHRASE SOURCES WITHOUT PLAGIARIZING

Summarize

When you summarize, you state the major ideas of an entire source or part of a source in a paragraph or perhaps even a sentence. The key is to put the summary in your own words. If you use words from the source, you must put those words within quotation marks.

Plagiarized

> Steven Johnson argues in *Interface Culture* that the concept of "surfing"
> is misapplied to the Internet because channel surfers hop back and forth
> between different channels because they're bored, but Web surfers click on
> links because they're interested. [Most of the words are lifted directly from
> the original; see pages 146–47.]

Acceptable Summary

> Steven Johnson argues in *Interface Culture* that the concept of "surfing" is
> misapplied to the Internet because users of the Web consciously choose to
> link to other sites while television viewers mindlessly flip through the chan-
> nels until something catches their attention.

Paraphrase

When you paraphrase, you represent the idea of the source in your
own words at about the same length as the original. You still need to
include the reference to the source of the idea. The following example
illustrates an unacceptable paraphrase.

Plagiarized

> Steven Johnson argues that the concept of "surfing" does a terrible injustice
> to what it means to navigate around the Web. What makes the idea of
> Web surfing infuriating is the association with television. Surfing is not a
> bad metaphor for channel hopping, but it doesn't fit what people do on the
> Web. Web surfing and channel surfing are truly different activities; to imag-
> ine them as the same is to ignore their defining characteristics. A channel
> surfer skips around because she's bored while a Web surfer clicks on a link
> because she's interested (107-09).

Even though the source is listed, this paraphrase is unacceptable. Too many of the words in the original are used directly here, including much of entire sentences. When a string of words is lifted from a source and inserted without quotation marks, the passage is plagiarized. Changing a few words in a sentence is not a paraphrase. Compare these two sentences:

Source

> Web surfing and channel surfing are genuinely different pursuits; to imagine them as equivalents is to ignore the defining characteristics of each medium.

Unacceptable Paraphrase

> Web surfing and channel surfing are truly different activities; to imagine them as the same is to ignore their defining characteristics.

The paraphrase takes the structure of the original sentence and substitutes a few words. It is much too similar to the original. A true paraphrase represents an entire rewriting of the idea from the source.

Acceptable Paraphrase

> Steven Johnson argues that "surfing" is a misleading term for describing how people navigate on the Web. He allows that "surfing" is appropriate for clicking across television channels because the viewer has to interact with what the networks and cable companies provide, just as the surfer has to interact with what the ocean provides. Web surfing, according to Johnson, operates at much greater depth and with much more consciousness of purpose. Web surfers actively follow links to make connections (107-09).

Even though this paraphrase contains a few words from the original, such as *navigate* and *connections*, these sentences are original in structure and wording while accurately conveying the meaning of the source.

INCORPORATE QUOTATIONS

Quotations are a frequent problem area in research papers. Review every quotation to ensure that each is used effectively and correctly, and follow these guidelines.

- Limit the use of long quotations. If you have more than one blocked quotation on a page, look closely to see if one or more can be paraphrased or summarized.

- Check that each quotation supports your major points rather than making major points for you. If the ideas rather than the original wording are what's important, paraphrase the quotation and cite the source.

- Check that each quotation is introduced and attributed. Each quotation should be introduced and the author or title named in a signal phrase: *Smith claims, Jones argues, Brown states.* (See the box on page 152 for a list of verbs that introduce quotations and paraphrases.)

- Check that each quotation is properly formatted and punctuated. Prose quotations longer than four lines should be indented one inch in MLA style. Shorter quotations should be enclosed within quotation marks.

- Check that you cite the source for each quotation. You are required to cite the sources of all direct quotations, paraphrases, and summaries.

- Check the accuracy of each quotation. It's easy to leave out words or to mistype a quotation. Compare what is in your paper to the original source. If you need to add words to make the quotation grammatical, make sure the added words are in brackets.

- Read your paper aloud to a classmate or a friend. Each quotation should flow smoothly when you read your paper aloud. Put a check beside rough spots as you read aloud so you can revise later.

**VERBS THAT INTRODUCE QUOTATIONS
AND PARAPHRASES**

acknowledge	conclude	note
add	contend	object
admit	criticize	observe
advise	declare	offer
agree	describe	point out
allow	disagree	refute
analyze	discuss	reject
answer	dispute	remark
argue	emphasize	reply
ask	explain	report
assert	express	respond
believe	find	show
charge	grant	state
claim	illustrate	suggest
comment	imply	think
compare	insist	write
complain	interpret	
concede	maintain	

DOCUMENTING SOURCES IN MLA STYLE

MLA stands for the Modern Language Association, and its style is the norm for the humanities and fine arts, including English and rhetoric and composition. If you have questions that this chapter does not address, consult the *MLA Handbook for Writers of Research Papers*, Seventh Edition (2009), and the *MLA Style Manual and Guide to Scholarly Publishing*, Third Edition (2008).

How to Cite a Source in Your Paper

Citing sources is a two-part process. When readers find a reference to a source (called an in-text or parenthetical citation) in the body of your paper, they can turn to the works-cited list at the end and find the full publication information. Place the author's last name and the page number inside parentheses at the end of the sentence.

> Anticipating the impact of Google's project of digitally scanning books in major research libraries, one observer predicts that "the real magic will come in the second act, as each word in each book is cross-linked, clustered, cited, extracted, indexed, analyzed, annotated, remixed, reassembled and woven deeper into the culture than ever before" (Kelly 43).

Author not
mentioned
in text

If you mention the author's name in the sentence, you do not have to put the name in the parenthetical reference at the end. Just cite the page number.

> Anticipating the impact of Google's project of digitally scanning books in major research libraries, Kevin Kelly predicts that "the real magic will come in the second act, as each word in each book is cross-linked, clustered, cited, extracted, indexed, analyzed, annotated, remixed, reassembled and woven deeper into the culture than ever before" (43).

Author
mentioned
in the text

The corresponding entry in the work-cited list at the end of your paper would be as follows.

> Works Cited
> Kelly, Kevin. "Scan This Book!" *New York Times* 14 May 2006, late ed., sec 6: 43+. Print.

Entry in
the works-
cited list

How to Cite an Entire Work, a Web Site, or Another Electronic Source

If you wish to cite an entire work (a book, a film, a performance, and so on), a Web site, or an electronic source that has no page numbers or paragraph numbers, MLA style instructs that you mention the name of the person (e.g., the author or director) in the text with a corresponding entry in the works-cited list. You do not need to include the author's name in parentheses. If you cannot identify the author, mention the title in your text.

Author mentioned in the text

> Joel Waldfogel discusses the implications of a study of alumni donations to colleges and universities, observing that parents give generously to top-rated colleges in the hope that their children's chances for admission will improve.

Works Cited

Waldfogel, Joel. "The Old College Try." *Slate*. Washington Post Newsweek Interactive, 6 July 2007. Web. 27 Jan. 2012.

Create an MLA-style Works-Cited List

To create your works-cited list, go through your paper and find every reference to the sources you consulted during your research. Each in-text reference must have an entry in your works-cited list.

Organize your works-cited list alphabetically by authors' last names or, if no author is listed, the first word in the title other than *a, an,* or *the.* (See pages 177–79 for a sample works-cited list.) MLA style uses four basic forms for entries in the works-cited list: books, periodicals (scholarly journals, newspapers, magazines), online library database sources, and other online sources (Web sites, discussion forums, blogs, online newspapers, online magazines, online government documents, and e-mail messages).

Works-Cited Entries for Books

Entries for books have three main elements.

Poster, Mark. *Information Please: Culture and Politics in the Age of Digital Machines.* Durham: Duke UP, 2006. Print.

1. Author's name.
- List the author's name with the last name first, followed by a period.

2. *Title of book.*
- Find the exact title on the title page, not the cover.
- Separate the title and subtitle with a colon.
- Italicize the title and put a period at the end.

3. Publication information.
- Give the city of publication and a colon.
- Give the name of the publisher, using accepted abbreviations.
- Give the date of publication.
- State the medium of publication (*Print*).

Works-Cited Entries for Periodicals

Entries for periodicals (scholarly journals, newspapers, magazines) have three main elements.

> MacDonald, Susan Peck. "The Erasure of Language." *College Composition and Communication* 58.4 (2007): 585-625. Print.

1. Author's name.
- List the author's name with the last name first, followed by a period.

2. "Title of article."
- Place the title of the article inside quotation marks.
- Insert a period before the closing quotation mark.

3. Publication information.
- Italicize the title of the journal.
- Give the volume and issue numbers.
- List the date of publication, in parentheses, followed by a colon.
- List the page numbers, followed by a period.
- Indicate the medium of publication (*Print*).

Works-Cited Entries for Library Database Sources

Basic entries for library database sources have four main elements.

Hede, Jesper. "Jews and Muslims in Dante's Vision." *European Review* 16.1
  (2008): 101-14. *Academic Search Premier.* Web. 14 Apr. 2012.

---

1. Author's name.
- List the author's name with the last name first, followed by a period.

2. "Title of article."
- Place the title of the article inside quotation marks.
- Insert a period before the closing quotation mark.

3. Print publication information.
- Give the print publication information in standard format, in this case for a periodical.

4. Database information.
- Italicize the name of the database, followed by a period.
- List the medium of publication, followed by a period. For all database sources, the medium of publication is *Web*.
- List the date you accessed the source (day, month, and year), followed by a period.

Works-Cited Entries for Other Online Sources

There are many formats for the different kinds of electronic publications. Here is the format of an entry for an online article.

Broudy, Oliver. "Air Head." *Salon.com.* Salon, 7 July 2007. Web. 6 Apr. 2012.

---

1. Author's name.
- List the author's name with the last name first, followed by a period.

2. "Title of work"; *Title of the overall Web site.*
- Place the title of work inside quotation marks if it is part of a larger Web site.

- Italicize the name of the overall site if it is different from the title of work.

- Some Web sites are updated, so list the version if you find it (e.g., *2012 ed.*).

3. Publication information.

- List the publisher or sponsor of the site followed by a comma. If not available, use *N.p.* (for *no publisher*).

- List the date of publication if available; if not, use *n.d.* (for *no date*).

- List the medium of publication (*Web*).

- List the date you accessed the source (day, month, and year).

MLA IN-TEXT CITATIONS

1. Author named in your text. Put the author's name in a signal phrase in your sentence.

> Sociologist Daniel Bell called this emerging U.S. economy the "postindustrial society" (3).

2. Author not named in your text. Put the author's last name and the page number inside parentheses at the end of the sentence.

> In 1997, the Gallup poll reported that 55% of adults in the United States think secondhand smoke is "very harmful," compared to only 36% in 1994 (Saad 4).

3. Work by a single author. The author's last name comes first, followed by the page number. There is no comma.

> (Bell 3)

4. Work by two or three authors. The authors' last names follow the order of the title page. If there are two authors, join the names with *and*.

If there are three authors, use commas between the first two names and a comma with *and* before the last name.

> (Francisco, Vaughn, and Lynn 7)

5. Work by four or more authors. You may use the phrase *et al.* (meaning "and others") for all names but the first, or you may write out all the names.

> (Abrams et al. 1653)

6. Work by an unnamed author. Use a shortened version of the title that includes at least the first important word. Your reader will use the shortened title to find the full title in the works-cited list.

> A review in the *New Yorker* of Ryan Adams's new album focuses on the artist's age ("Pure" 25).

7. Work by a group or organization. Treat the group or organization as the author, but try to identify the group author in the text and place only the page number in the parentheses. Shorten terms that are commonly abbreviated.

> According to the *Irish Free State Handbook*, published by the Ministry for Industry and Finance, the population of Ireland in 1929 was approximately 4,192,000 (23).

8. Quotations longer than four lines. When using indented (block) quotations of more than four lines, place the period *before* the parentheses enclosing the page number.

In her article "Art for Everybody," Susan Orlean attempts to explain the popularity of painter Thomas Kinkade:

> People like to own things they think are valuable....The high
> price of limited editions is part of their appeal: it implies that they
> are choice and exclusive, and that only a certain class of people
> will be able to afford them—a limited edition of people with taste
> and discernment. (128)

This same statement could possibly also explain the popularity of phenomena
like PBS's *Antiques Road Show*.

**9. Web sources including Web pages, blogs, podcasts, wikis, videos,
and other multimedia sources.** Give the author in the text instead of
putting the author's name in parentheses.

Andrew Keen ironically used his own blog to claim that "blogs are boring to
write (yawn), boring to read (yawn), and boring to discuss (yawn)."

If you cannot identify the author, mention the title in your text.

The podcast "Catalina's Cubs" describes the excitement on Catalina Island
when the Chicago Cubs went there for spring training in the 1940s.

10. Work in an anthology. Cite the name of the author of the work within
an anthology, not the name of the editor of the collection. Alphabetize
the entry in the list of works cited by the author, not the editor.

In "Beard," Melissa Jane Hardie explores the role assumed by Elizabeth
Taylor as the celebrity companion of gay actors including Rock Hudson and
Montgomery Cliff (278-79).

11. Two or more works by the same author. When an author has two
or more items in the works-cited list, distinguish which work you are

citing by using the author's last name and then a shortened version of the title of each source.

> The majority of books written about coauthorship focus on partners of the same sex (Laird, *Women* 351).

12. Different authors with the same last name. If your list of works cited contains items by two or more different authors with the same last name, include the initial of the first name in the parenthetical reference.

> Web surfing requires more mental involvement than channel surfing (S. Johnson 107).

13. Two or more sources within the same sentence. Place each citation directly after the statement it supports.

> In the 1990s, many sweeping pronouncements were made that the Internet is the best opportunity to improve education since the printing press (Ellsworth xxii) or even in the history of the world (Dyrli and Kinnaman 79).

14. Two or more sources within the same citation. If two sources support a single point, separate them with a semicolon.

> (McKibbin 39; Gore 92)

15. Work quoted in another source. When you do not have access to the original source of the material you wish to use, put the abbreviation *qtd. in* (quoted in) before the information about the indirect source.

> National governments have become increasingly what Ulrich Beck, in a 1999 interview, calls "zombie institutions"—institutions that are "dead and still alive" (qtd. in Bauman 6).

MLA WORKS-CITED LIST: BOOKS

16. Book by one author.

Doctorow, E. L. *The March*. New York: Random, 2005. Print.

17. Two or more books by the same author. In the entry for the first book, include the author's name. In the second entry, substitute three hyphens and a period for the author's name. List the titles of books by the same author in alphabetical order.

Grimsley, Jim. *Boulevard*. Chapel Hill: Algonquin, 2002. Print.

—. *Dream Boy*. New York: Simon, 1995. Print.

18. Book by two or three authors. Second and subsequent authors' names appear first name first. A comma separates the authors' names.

Chapkis, Wendy, and Richard J. Webb. *Dying to Get High: Marijuana as Medicine*. New York: New York UP, 2008. Print.

19. Book by four or more authors. You may use the phrase *et al.* for all authors but the first, or you may write out all the names. Use the same method in the in-text citation as you do in the works-cited list.

Zukin, Cliff, et al. *A New Engagement? Political Participation, Civic Life, and the Changing American Citizen*. New York: Oxford UP, 2006. Print.

20. Book by an unknown author. Begin the entry with the title.

Encyclopedia of Americana. New York: Somerset, 2001. Print.

21. Book by a group or organization. Treat the group as the author of the work.

> United Nations. *The Charter of the United Nations: A Commentary.* New York: Oxford UP, 2000. Print.

22. Introduction, foreword, preface, or afterword. Give the author and then the name of the specific part being cited. Next, name the book. Then, if the author for the whole work is different, put that author's name after the word *By.* Place inclusive page numbers at the end.

> Benstock, Sheri. Introduction. *The House of Mirth.* By Edith Wharton. Boston: Bedford-St. Martin's, 2002. 3-24. Print.

23. Single chapter written by same author as the book.

> Ardis, Ann L. "Mapping the Middlebrow in Edwardian England." *Modernism and Cultural Conflict: 1880-1922.* Cambridge: Cambridge UP, 2002. 114–42. Print.

24. Selection from an anthology or edited collection.

> Sedaris, David. "Full House." *The Best American Nonrequired Reading 2004.* Ed. Dave Eggers. Boston: Houghton, 2004. 350-58. Print.

25. Book with an editor. List an edited book under the editor's name if your focus is on the editor. Otherwise, cite an edited book under the author's name as shown in the second example.

> Lewis, Gifford, ed. *The Big House of Inver.* By Edith Somerville and Martin Ross. Dublin: Farmar, 2000. Print.
>
> Somerville, Edith and Martin Ross. *The Big House of Inver.* Ed. Gifford Lewis. Dublin: Farmar, 2000. Print.

26. Book with a translator.

Benjamin, Walter. *The Arcades Project*. Trans. Howard Eiland and Kevin McLaughlin. Cambridge: Harvard UP, 1999. Print.

27. Second or subsequent edition of a book.

Hawthorn, Jeremy, ed. *A Concise Glossary of Contemporary Literary Theory*. 3rd ed. London: Arnold, 2001. Print.

MLA WORKS-CITED LIST: PERIODICALS

28. Journal article by one author.

Mallory, Anne. "Burke, Boredom, and the Theater of Counterrevolution." *PMLA* 118.2 (2003): 224-38. Print.

29. Journal article by two or three authors.

Miller, Thomas P., and Brian Jackson. "What Are English Majors For?" *College Composition and Communication* 58.4 (2007): 682-708. Print.

30. Journal article by four or more authors. You may use the phrase *et al.* for all authors but the first, or you may write out all the names.

Breece, Katherine E. et al. "Patterns of mtDNA Diversity in Northwestern North America." *Human Biology* 76.5 (2004): 33-54. Print.

31. Article in a scholarly journal. List the volume and issue numbers after the name of the journal.

Duncan, Mike. "Whatever Happened to the Paragraph?" *College English* 69.5 (2007): 470-95. Print.

32. Article in a scholarly journal that uses only issue numbers. List the issue number after the name of the journal.

McCall, Sophie. "Double Vision Reading." *Canadian Literature* 194 (2007): 95-97. Print.

33. Monthly or seasonal magazines. Use the month (or season) and year in place of the volume. Abbreviate the names of all months except May, June, and July.

Barlow, John Perry. "Africa Rising: Everything You Know about Africa Is Wrong." *Wired* Jan. 1998: 142-58. Print.

34. Weekly or biweekly magazines. Give both the day and the month of publication, as listed on the issue.

Brody, Richard. "A Clash of Symbols." *New Yorker* 25 June 2007: 16. Print.

35. Newspaper article by one author.

Marriott, Michel. "Arts and Crafts for the Digital Age." *New York Times* 8 June 2006, late ed.: C13. Print.

36. Article by two or three authors.

Schwirtz, Michael, and Joshua Yaffa. "A Clash of Cultures at a Square in Moscow." *New York Times* 11 July 2007, late ed.: A9. Print.

37. Newspaper article by an unknown author. Begin the entry with the title.

"The Dotted Line." *Washington Post* 8 June 2006, final ed.: E2. Print.

REVIEWS, EDITORIALS, LETTERS TO THE EDITOR

38. Review. If there is no title, just name the work reviewed.

> Mendelsohn, Daniel. "The Two Oscar Wildes." Rev. of *The Importance of Being Earnest*, dir. Oliver Parker. *The New York Review of Books* 10 Oct. 2002: 23-24. Print.

39. Editorial.

> "Hush-hush, Sweet Liberty." Editorial. *Los Angeles Times* 7 July 2007: A18. Print.

40. Letter to the editor.

> Doyle, Joe. Letter. *Direct* 1 July 2007: 48. Print.

MLA WORKS-CITED LIST: LIBRARY DATABASE SOURCES

41. Work from a library database. Begin with the print publication information, then the name of the database (italicized), the medium (*Web*), and the date of access (day, month, and year).

> Snider, Michael. "Wired to Another World." *Maclean's* 3 Mar. 2003: 23-24. *Academic Search Premier*. Web. 14 Feb. 2012.

MLA WORKS-CITED LIST: WEB SOURCES

When Do You List a URL?

MLA style no longer requires including URLs of Web sources in reference citations. URLs are of limited value because they change frequently and they can be specific to an individual search. Include the

URL as supplementary information only when your readers probably cannot locate the source without the URL.

42. Publication by a known author.

> Boerner, Steve. "Leopold Mozart." *The Mozart Project: Biography*. Mozart Project, 21 Mar. 1998. Web. 30 Oct. 2011.

43. Publication by a group or organization. If a work has no author's or editor's name listed, begin the entry with the title.

> "State of the Birds." *Audubon*. National Audubon Society, 2008. Web. 19 Aug. 2012.

44. Article in a scholarly journal on the Web. Some scholarly journals are published on the Web only. List articles by author, title, name of journal in italics, volume and issue number, and year of publication. If the journal does not have page numbers, use *n. pag.* in place of page numbers. Then list the medium of publication (*Web*) and the date of access (day, month, and year).

> Fleckenstein, Kristie. "Who's Writing? Aristotelian Ethos and the Author Position in Digital Poetics." *Kairos* 11.3 (2007): n. pag. Web. 6 Apr. 2012.

45. Article in a newspaper on the Web. The first date is the date of publication; the second is the date of access.

> Brown, Patricia Leigh. "Australia in Sonoma." *New York Times*. New York Times, 5 July 2008. Web. 3 Aug. 2012.

46. Article in a magazine on the Web.

> Brown, Patricia Leigh. "The Wild Horse Is Us." *Newsweek*. Newsweek, 1 July 2008. Web. 12 Dec. 2011.

47. Book on the Web.

Prebish, Charles S. and Kenneth K. Tanaka. *The Faces of Buddhism in America*. Berkeley: U of California P, 2003. *eScholarship Editions*. Web. 2 May 2012.

48. Wiki entry. Wiki content is written collaboratively, thus no author is listed. Because the content on Wiki changes frequently, Wikis are not considered as reliable scholarly sources.

"Snowboard." *Wikipedia*. Wikimedia Foundation, 2012. Web. 30 Jan. 2012.

49. Podcast.

Sussingham, Robin. "All Things Autumn." No. 2. *HighLifeUtah*. N.p., 20 Nov. 2006. Web. 28 Feb. 2012.

50. PDFs and digital files. PDFs and other digital files often can be downloaded through links. Determine the kind of work you are citing, include the appropriate information for the particular kind of work, and list the type of file.

Glaser, Edward L., and Albert Saiz. "The Rise of the Skilled City." Discussion Paper No. 2025. Harvard Institute of Economic Research. Cambridge: Harvard U., 2003. PDF file.

51. Blog entry. If there is no sponsor or publisher for the blog, use *N.p.*

Arrington, Michael. "Think Before You Voicemail." *TechCrunch*. N.p., 5 July 2008. Web. 10 Sept. 2012.

52. Video on the Web. Video on the Web often lacks a creator and a date. Begin the entry with a title if you cannot find a creator. Use *n.d.* if you cannot find a date.

Wesch, Michael. *A Vision of Students Today. YouTube.* YouTube, 2007. Web. 28 May 2012.

53. Personal home page. List *Home page* without quotation marks in place of the title. If no date is listed, use *n.d.*

Graff, Harvey J. Home page. Dept. of English, Ohio State U, n.d. Web. 15 Nov. 2012.

MLA WORKS-CITED LIST: OTHER SOURCES

54. E-mail. Give the name of the writer, the subject line, a description of the message, the date, and the medium of delivery (*E-mail*).

Ballmer, Steve. "A New Era of Business Productivity and Innovation." Message to Microsoft Executive E-mail. 30 Nov. 2006. E-mail.

55. Sound recording.

McCoury, Del, perf. "1952 Vincent Black Lightning." By Richard Thompson. *Del and the Boys.* Ceili, 2001. CD.

56. Film. Begin with the title in italics. List the director, the distributor, the date, and the medium. Other data, such as the names of the screen-writers and performers, is optional.

Wanted. Dir. Timur Bekmambetov. Perf. James McAvoy, Angelina Jolie, and Morgan Freeman. Universal, 2008. Film.

57. DVD.

No Country for Old Men. Dir. Joel Coen and Ethan Coen. Perf. Tommy Lee Jones, Javier Bardem, and Josh Brolin. Paramount, 2007. DVD.

58. Television or radio program.

"Garage Sale." *The Office.* Perf. Steve Carrell. NBC. 24 Mar. 2011. Television.

SAMPLE MLA PAPER

MLA style does not require a title page. Ask your instructor whether you need one.

Witkowski 1

Include your last name and page number as page header, beginning with the first page, 1/2" from the top.

Brian Witkowski

Professor Mendelsohn

RHE 309K

3 May 2010

Need a Cure for Tribe Fever?

How About a Dip in the Lake?

Everyone is familiar with the Cleveland Indians' Chief Wahoo logo—and I do mean everyone, not just Clevelanders. Across America people wear the smil-ing mascot on Cleveland Indians caps and jerseys, and recent trends in sports merchandise have popularized new groovy multicolored Indians sportswear. Because of lucrative contracts between major league baseball and Little League, youth teams all over the country don Cleveland's famous (or infamous) smiling Indian each season as fresh-faced kids scamper onto the diamonds looking like mini major leaguers (Liu). Various incarna-tions of the famous Chief Wahoo—described by writer Ryan Zimmerman as "a grotesque caricature grinning idiotically through enormous bucked teeth"—have been around since the 1940s. Now redder and even more car-toonish than the original hook-nosed, beige Indian with a devilish grin, Wahoo often passes as a cheerful base-ball buddy like the San Diego Chicken or the St. Louis Cardinals' Fredbird.

Though defined by its distinctive logo, Cleveland baseball far preceded its famous mascot. The team changed from the Forest Citys to the Spiders to the Bluebirds/Blues to the Broncos to the Naps and finally

Use 1" margins all around. Double-space everything.

Cite publications by the name of the author (or authors).

Center your title. Do not put the title in quotation marks or type it in all capital letters.

Indent each paragraph 1/2" on the ruler.

to the Indians. Dubbed the Naps in 1903 in honor of
its star player and manager Napoleon Lajoie, the team
gained their current appellation in 1915. After Lajoie
was traded, the team's president challenged sportswrit-
ers to devise a suitable "temporary" label for the floundering club. Publicity material claims that the writers
decided on the Indians to celebrate Louis Sockalexis, a
Penobscot Indian who played for the team from 1897 to
1899. With a high batting average and the notability of
being the first Native American in professional baseball,
Sockalexis was immortalized by the new Cleveland label
(Schneider 10-23). (Contrary to popular lore, some cite
alternative—and less reverent—motivations behind the
team's naming and point to a lack of Sockalexis publicity in period newspaper articles discussing the team's
naming process [Staurowsky 95-97].) Almost ninety
years later, the "temporary" name continues to raise
eyebrows, in both its marketability and its ideological
questionability.

Today the logo is more than a little embarrassing.
Since the high-profile actions of the American Indian
Movement (AIM) in the 1970s, sports teams around the
country—including the Indians—have been criticized
for their racially insensitive mascots. Native American
groups question these caricatured icons—not just because
of grossly stereotyped mascots, but also because of what
visual displays of team support say about Native American
culture. Across the country, professional sporting teams,
as well as high schools and colleges, perform faux rituals
in the name of team spirit. As Tim Giago, publisher of *The*

Lakota Times, a weekly South Dakotan Native American newspaper, has noted,

> The sham rituals, such as the wearing of feathers, smoking of so-called peace pipes, beating of tomtoms, fake dances, horrendous attempts at singing Indian songs, the so-called war whoops, and the painted faces, address more than the issues of racism. They are direct attacks upon the spirituality of the Indian people. (qtd. in Wulf)

Controversy over such performances still fuels the fire between activists and alumni at schools such as the University of Illinois at Champaign-Urbana, where during many decades of football halftimes fans cheered the performance of a student (often white) dressed as Chief Illiniwek. In March of 2007, the University of Illinois board of trustees voted in a nearly unanimous decision to retire the mascot's name, regalia, and image ("Illinois").

Since 1969, when Oklahoma disavowed its "Little Red" mascot, more than 600 school and minor league teams have followed a more ethnically sensitive trend and ditched their "tribal" mascots (Price). High-profile teams such as Stanford, St. John's University, and Miami (Ohio) University have changed their team names from the Indians to the Cardinal (1972), the Redmen to the Red Storm (1993), and the Redskins to the Redhawks (1996), respectively. In 2005, the NCAA officially ruled that "colleges whose nicknames or mascots refer to American Indians will not be permitted to hold National Collegiate Athletic Association tournament events" (Wolverton). By

Witkowski 4

September 2005, only seventeen schools remained in violation (Wolverton). While many people see such controversies as mere bowing to the pressures of the late twentieth
and early twenty-first centuries, others see the mascot issue
as a topic well worthy of debate.

Cleveland's own Chief Wahoo has far from avoided
controversy. Multiple conflicts between Wahoo devotees and
dissenters occur annually during the baseball season. At the
opening game of 1995, fifty Native Americans and supporters took stations around Jacobs Field to demonstrate against
the use of the cartoonish smiling crimson mascot (Kropk).
Arrests were made in 1998 when demonstrators from the
United Church of Christ burned a three-foot Chief Wahoo
doll in effigy ("Judge"). Opinions on the mascot remain
mixed. Jacoby Ellsbury, outfielder for the Boston Red Sox
and a member of the Colorado River Indian Tribes, said in
2007, "I'm not offended [by the mascot]. You can look at
it two different ways. You can look at it that it's offensive
or you can look at it that they are representing Native
Americans. Usually I'll try to take the positive out of it"
(Shaughnessy). Nonetheless, Ellsbury still acknowledges that
he "can see both sides of [the controversy]" (Shaughnessy).
Wedded to their memorabilia, fans proudly stand behind their
Indian as others lobby vociferously for its removal, splitting
government officials, fans, and social and religious groups.

In 2000 Cleveland mayor Michael White came out
publicly against the team mascot, joining an already established group of religious leaders, laypersons, and civil rights
activists who had demanded Wahoo's retirement. African
American religious and civic leaders such as Rev. Gregory

Witkowski 5

A. Jacobs pointed to the absurdity of minority groups who embrace the Wahoo symbol. "Each of us has had to fight its [sic] own battle, quite frankly," Jacobs stated. "We cannot continue to live in this kind of hypocrisy that says, Yes, we are in solidarity with my [sic] brothers and sisters, yet we continue to exploit them" (qtd. in Briggs).

This controversy also swirls outside of the greater Cleveland area. In 2009 the image of Wahoo was removed from the team's training complex in Goodyear, Arizona ("Cleveland"), while the *Seattle Times* went so far as to digitally remove the Wahoo symbol from images of the Cleveland baseball cap ("Newspaper"). As other teams make ethnically sensitive and image-conscious choices to change their mascots, Cleveland stands firm in its resolve to retain Chief Wahoo. Despite internal division and public ridicule fueled by the team icon, the city refuses to budge.

Cleveland's stubbornness on the issue of Wahoo runs contrary to the city's recently improved image and downtown revitalization. As a native of Cleveland, I understand the power of "Tribe Fever" and the unabashed pride one feels when wearing Wahoo garb during a winning (or losing) season. Often it is not until we leave northeastern Ohio that we realize the negative image that Wahoo projects. What then can Cleveland do to simultaneously save face and bolster its burgeoning positive city image? I propose that the team finally change the "temporary" Indians label. In a city so proud of its diverse ethnic heritage—African American, Italian American, and Eastern European American to name a few examples— why stand as a bearer of retrograde ethnic politics? Cleveland should take this opportunity to link its positive Midwestern image to the team of which it is so proud. I propose changing the team's name to the Cleveland Lakers.

The city's revival in the last twenty years has embraced the geographic and aesthetic grandeur of Lake Erie. Disavowing its "mistake on the lake" moniker of the late 1970s, Cleveland has traded aquatic pollution fires for a booming lakeside business district. Attractions such as the Great Lakes Science Center, the Rock and Roll Hall of Fame, and the new Cleveland Browns Stadium take advantage of the beauty of the landscape and take back the lake. Why not continue this trend through one of the city's biggest and highest-profile moneymakers: professional baseball? By changing the team's name to the Lakers, the city would gain national advertisement for one of its major selling points, while simultaneously announcing a new ethnically inclusive image that is appropriate to our wonderfully diverse city. It would be a public relations triumph for the city.

Of course this call will be met with many objections. Why do we have to buckle to pressure? Do we not live in a free country? What fans and citizens alike need to keep in mind is that ideological pressures would not be the sole motivation for this move. Yes, retiring Chief Wahoo would take Cleveland off AIM's hit list. Yes, such a move would promote a kinder and gentler Cleveland. At the same time, however, such a gesture would work toward uniting the community. So much civic division exists over this issue that a renaming could help start to heal these old wounds.

Additionally, this type of change could bring added economic prosperity to the city. First, a change in

name will bring a new wave of team merchandise. Licensed
sports apparel generates more than a 10-billion-dollar
annual retail business in the United States, and teams have
proven repeatedly that new uniforms and logos can provide
new capital. After all, a new logo for the Seattle Mariners
bolstered severely slumping merchandise sales (Lefton).
Wahoo devotees need not panic; the booming vintage
uniform business will keep him alive, as is demonstrated
by the current ability to purchase replica 1940s jerseys
with the old Indians logo. Also, good press created by this
change will hopefully help increase tourism in Cleveland.
If the goodwill created by the Cleveland Lakers can prove
half as profitable as the Rock and Roll Hall of Fame, then
local businesses will be humming a happy tune. Finally, if
history repeats itself, a change to a more culturally inclusive logo could, in and of itself, prove to be a cash cow.
When Miami University changed from the Redskins to
the Redhawks, it saw alumni donations skyrocket (Price).
A less divisive mascot would prove lucrative to the ball
club, the city, and the players themselves. (Sluggers with
inoffensive logos make excellent spokesmen.)

Perhaps this proposal sounds far-fetched: Los
Angeles may seem to have cornered the market on Lakers.
But where is their lake? (The Lakers were formerly the
Minneapolis Lakers, where the name makes sense in the
"Land of 10,000 Lakes.") Various professional and col-
legiate sports teams—such as baseball's San Francisco
Giants and football's New York Giants—share a team
name, so licensing should not be an issue. If Los Angeles
has qualms about sharing the name, perhaps Cleveland

Witkowski 8

could persuade Los Angeles to become the Surfers or the
Stars; after all, Los Angeles players seem to spend as much
time on the big and small screens as on the court.

   Now is the perfect time for Cleveland to make this
jump. Perhaps a new look will help usher in a new era
of Cleveland baseball and a World Series ring to boot.
Through various dry spells, the Cleveland Indians institution has symbolically turned to the descendants of
Sockalexis, asking for goodwill or a latter-generation
Penobscot slugger (Fleitz 3). Perhaps the best way to win
goodwill, fortunes, and the team's first World Series title
since 1948 would be to eschew a grinning life-size Chief
Wahoo for the new Cleveland Laker, an oversized furry
monster sporting water wings, cleats, and a catcher's mask.
His seventh-inning-stretch show could include an air-guitar
solo with a baseball bat as he quietly reminds everyone that
the Rock Hall is just down the street.

Witkowski 9

Works Cited

Center "Works Cited" on a new page.

Briggs, David. "Churches Go to Bat Against Chief
   Wahoo." *Cleveland Plain Dealer* 25 Aug. 2000:
   1A. *LexisNexis Academic*. Web. 19 Apr. 2010.

"Cleveland Indians' Chief Wahoo Logo Left Off Team's
   Ballpark, Training Complex in Goodyear, Arizona."
   Cleveland.com. Cleveland Plain Dealer, 12 Apr. 2009.
   Web. 23 Apr. 2010.

Double-space all entries. Indent all but the first line in each entry one-half inch.

Fleitz, David L. *Louis Sockalexis: The First Cleveland Indian*. Jefferson: McFarland, 2002. Print.

"Illinois Trustees Vote to Retire Chief Illiniwek." *ESPN*. ESPN Internet Ventures, 13 Mar. 2007. Web. 26 Apr. 2010.

"Judge Dismisses Charges Against City in Wahoo Protest." *Associated Press* 6 Aug. 2001. *LexisNexis Academic*. Web. 19 Apr. 2010.

Kropk, M. R. "Chief Wahoo Protestors Largely Ignored by Fans." *Austin American Statesman* 6 May 1995: D4. Print.

Lefton, Terry. "Looks Are Everything: For New Franchises, Licensing Battles Must Be Won Long Before the Team Even Takes the Field." *Sport* 89 (May 1998): 32. Print.

Liu, Caitlin. "Bawl Game." *Portfolio.com*. Condé Nast, 21 Oct. 2008. Web. 28 Apr. 2009.

"Newspaper Edits Cleveland Indian Logo from Cap Photo." *Associated Press* 31 Mar. 1997. *LexisNexis Academic*. Web. 27 Apr. 2010.

Price, S. L. "The Indian Wars." *Sports Illustrated* 4 Mar. 2002: 66+. *Academic OneFile*. Web. 20 Apr. 2010.

Schneider, Russell. *The Cleveland Indians Encyclopedia*. Philadelphia: Temple UP, 1996. Print.

Shaughnessy, Dan. "They've Had Some Chief Concerns." *Boston Globe* 12 October. 2007: C5. *LexisNexis Academic*. Web. 19 Apr. 2010.

Staurowsky, Ellen J. "Sockalexis and the Making of the Myth at the Core of the Cleveland's 'Indian' Image." *Team Spirits: The Native American Mascots*

Alphabetize entries by the last names of the authors or by the first important word in the title if no author is listed.

Italicize the titles of books and periodicals.

Check to make sure all the sources you have cited in your text are in the list of works cited.

Witkowski 11

Controversy. Eds. C. Richard King and Charles
Fruehling Springwood. Lincoln: U of Nebraska P,
2001. 82-106. Print.

Wolverton, Brad. "NCAA Restricts Colleges With
Indian Nicknames and Mascots." *Chronicle of
Higher Education* 2 Sept. 2005: A65. *ProQuest.*
Web. 25 Apr. 2010.

Wulf, Steve. "A Brave Move." *Sports Illustrated* 24 Feb.
1992: 7. Print.

Zimmerman, Ryan. "The Cleveland Indians' Mascot
Must Go." *Christian Science Monitor* 15 Oct. 2007:
5. *LexisNexis Academic.* Web. 19 Apr. 2010.

7

Revising an Argument

Writing is not an assembly-line process of finding ideas, writing a draft, and revising, editing, and proofreading the draft, all in that order. While you write and revise, you will often think of additional reasons to support your position. Likely you will work through your paper or project in multiple drafts, strengthening your content, organization, and readability in each successive draft.

EVALUATE YOUR DRAFT

To review and evaluate your draft, pretend you are someone who is either uninformed about your subject or informed but likely to disagree with you. If possible, think of an actual person and imagine yourself as that person. Read your draft aloud all the way through. When you read aloud, you often hear clunky phrases and catch errors, but just put checks in the margins so you can return to them later. You don't want to get bogged down with the little stuff. What you are after in this stage is an overall sense of how well you accomplished what you set out to do. Use the questions in the box below to evaluate your draft. Note any places where you might make improvements.

CHECKLIST FOR EVALUATING YOUR DRAFT

Does your paper or project meet the assignment?

- Look again at your assignment, especially at key words such as *define*, *analyze causes*, *evaluate*, and *propose*. Does your paper or project do what the assignment requires? If not, how can you change it?
- Look again at the assignment for specific guidelines including length, format, and amount of research. Does your work meet these guidelines?

Can you better focus your thesis and your supporting reasons?

- You may have started out with a large topic and ended up writing about one aspect of it. Can you make your thesis even more precise?
- Can you find the exact location where you link each reason to your thesis?

Are your main points adequately developed?

- Can you explain your reasons in more detail?
- Can you add evidence to better support your main points?
- Do you provide enough background on your topic?

Is your organization effective?

- Is the order of your main points clear? (You may want to make a quick outline of your draft if you have not done so already.)
- Are there any abrupt shifts or gaps?
- Are there sections or paragraphs that should be rearranged?

Are your key terms adequately defined?

- What are your key terms?
- Can you define these terms more precisely?

Do you consider other points of view?

- Where do you acknowledge views besides your own? If you don't acknowledge other views, where can you add them?
- How can you make your discussion of opposing views more acceptable to readers who hold those views?

Do you represent yourself effectively?

- Forget for the moment that you wrote what you are reading. What is your impression of the writer?
- Is the tone of the writing appropriate for the subject?

Can you improve your title and introduction?

- Can you make your title more specific and indicate your stance?
- Can you think of a way to start faster and to get your readers interested in what you have to say?

Can you improve your conclusion?

- Can you think of an example that sums up your position?
- Can you discuss an implication of your argument that will make your readers think more about the subject?
- If you are writing a proposal, can you end with a call for action?

Can you improve your visual presentation?

- Is the type font easy to read and consistent?
- Would headings and subheadings help to mark the major sections of your argument?
- If you have statistical data, do you use charts?
- Would illustrations, maps, or other graphics help to explain your main points?

When you finish, make a list of your goals for the revision. You may have to write another draft before you move to the next stage.

RESPOND TO THE WRITING OF OTHERS

Your instructor may ask you to respond to the drafts of your classmates. Responding to other people's writing requires the same careful attention you give to your own draft. To write a helpful response, you should go through the draft more than once.

First Reading

Read at your normal rate the first time through without stopping. When you finish, you should have a clear sense of what the writer is trying to accomplish. Try writing the following:

- **Main idea and purpose:** Write a sentence that summarizes what you think is the writer's main idea in the draft.
- **Purpose:** Write a sentence that states what you think the writer is trying to accomplish in the draft.

Second Reading

In your second reading, you should be most concerned with the content, organization, and completeness of the draft. Make notes in pencil as you read.

- **Introduction:** Does the writer's first paragraph effectively introduce the topic and engage your interest?

- **Thesis:** What exactly is the writer's thesis? Is it clear? Note in the margin where you think the thesis is located.

- **Focus:** Does the writer maintain focus on the thesis? Note any places where the writer seems to wander off to another topic.

- **Organization:** Are the sections and paragraphs arranged effectively? Do any paragraphs seem to be out of place? Can you suggest a better order for the paragraphs?

- **Completeness:** Are there sections or paragraphs that lack key information or adequate development? Where do you want to know more?

- **Conclusion:** Does the last paragraph wrap up the discussion in a way that leaves the reader satisfied? Is it thought-provoking and memorable?

- **Sources:** Are outside sources cited accurately? Are quotations used correctly and worked into the fabric of the draft?

Third Reading

In your third reading, turn your attention to matters of audience, style, and tone.

- **Audience:** Who are the writer's intended readers? What does the writer assume the audience knows and believes?

- **Style:** Does the writer have sentences that are accurate and emphasize the subject of the paragraph? Can any sentences be eliminated or combined?

- **Tone:** Is the tone appropriate for the writer's purpose and audience? Is the tone consistent throughout the draft? Are there places where another word or phrase might work better?

When you have finished the third reading, write a short paragraph on each bulleted item above. Refer to specific paragraphs in the draft by number. Then end by answering these two questions:

- What does the writer do especially well in the draft?
- What one or two things would most improve the draft in a revision?

EDIT AND PROOFREAD CAREFULLY

When you finish revising, you are ready for one final careful reading with the goals of improving your style and eliminating errors.

Edit for Style

- **Check connections between sentences and paragraphs.** Notice how your sentences flow within each paragraph and from paragraph to paragraph. If you need to signal the relationship from one sentence or paragraph to the next, use a transitional word or phrase (e.g., *in addition, moreover, similarly, however, nevertheless*).

- **Check your sentences.** Often you will pick up problems with individual sentences by reading aloud. If you notice that a sentence doesn't sound right, think about how you might rephrase it. If a sentence seems too long, consider breaking it into two or more sentences. If you notice a string of short sentences that sound choppy, consider combining them.

- **Eliminate wordiness.** Look for wordy expressions such as *because of the fact that* and *at this point in time*, which can easily be shortened to *because* and *now*. Reduce unnecessary repetition such as *attractive in appearance* or *visible to the eye* to *attractive* and *visible*. Remove unnecessary words like *very, really,* and *totally*. See how many words you can remove without losing the meaning.

- **Use active verbs.** Make your style more lively by replacing forms of *be* (*is, are, was, were*) or verbs ending in *–ing* with active verbs. Sentences that begin with *There is (are)* and *It is* can often be rewritten with active verbs.

Proofread Carefully

In your final pass through your text, eliminate as many errors as you can. To become an effective proofreader, you have to learn to slow down. Some writers find that moving from word to word with a pencil slows them down enough to find errors. Others read backward to force them to concentrate on each word.

- **Know what your spelling checker can and can't do.** Spelling checkers are the greatest invention since peanut butter. They turn up many typos and misspellings that are hard to catch. But spelling checkers do not catch wrong words (*to much* for *too much*), missing endings (*three dog*), and other similar errors.

- **Check for grammar and punctuation.** Nothing hurts your credibility more than leaving errors in what you write. Many job and professional school applications get tossed in the reject pile because of a single, glaring error. Readers probably shouldn't make such harsh judgments when they find errors, but in fact they do. Keep a grammar handbook beside your computer, and use it when you are uncertain about what is correct.

Index